June 5, 1943

Dear Mother and Dad,

Well, they keep telling me I am a soldier now. We got there about two o'clock yesterday...

Dear Mother and Dad
A WWII Soldier's Letters Home

of the afternoon. After supper we learned how to make beds and finally got three aptitude tests. The results were listed on one of the cards during our processing today. On the first general aptitude test (IQ) I got a 141 (Not Bad). Ernie said I needed 115 to be able to receive engineering training. The next test was the radio receiving aptitude. The only thing you could do was guess on answers so I got an 85 out of a possible 150. The last test was right up my alley. I got a 148 out of 150 on this mechanical aptitude quiz.

Compiled by Donald Barrett Vail, Jr.

Today we got our uniforms and three shots in the arm. We have to wear the fatigue outfits most of the time. As usual I fainted for half a minute after the three shots were in. This afternoon we saw training films except for the excessive heat.

For my sisters,
Diane, Cynthia and Shelley
and my children,
Hannah and Isaac

Introduction
A Soldier's Letters Home

Meet Donald...

My father, Donald Barrett Vail, was born December 23, 1923 to Harvey (1887-1970) and Mildred Vail (1897-1997) in Dunellen, New Jersey. He was their only child. Harvey came from a long line of Quakers. Mildred was a Baptist. As a conscientious objector to combat in World War I, Harvey worked at an Evacuation Hospital for the occupation forces in Coblenz, Germany. After the war he worked as a clerk in the Factory Office of the Wood Newspaper Machinery Corporation in Plainfield, New Jersey. Mildred was a homemaker. She was also very civic-minded as the following letters will reveal.

In his youth, Donald applied himself well to school and earned his way into the Honor Society in high school. He excelled in the sciences and math but did average work in English. He enjoyed making model airplanes and collected pictures of prototypical aircraft. He also enjoyed model railroading, making his own models of train cars and engines. His after school job as a teenager was at the Model Railroad Shop near his home on Vail Avenue.

Following high school, Donald entered Newark College of Engineering (NCE) to pursue a degree in Mechanical Engineering. At the point that he joined the Army, he had completed two years toward that degree.

Donald entered World War II as a private in the U.S. Army June 4, 1943. His basic training was completed at Fort Custer in Michigan where he received instruction for the Military Police Escort Guard (MPEG). As an MPEG he served at a Prisoner of War Camp in Concordia, Kansas from August to December, 1943. During this time, he served at a side location called the Agricultural Experiment Station at Ft. Hays State College in Hays, Kansas. The German Prisoners of War from Concordia were engaged to work on projects for local farmers there. The MPEG gave oversight to the transportation and work of these prisoners.

The next phase of his service came as he was accepted into the Army Specialized Training Program (ASTP). This program, created to meet "the exigencies of war," included developing the Army's manpower supply while training soldiers to meet the technological challenges of the war. In Donald's case, the training he received was an extension of his previous college work in engineering with specific training related to the engineering needs of the time. He completed this work at the University of Tennessee.

He also received training in the infantry where he was qualified as a marksman at Camp Atterbury, Indiana. Following that, he was given a course in mechanics at the Atlanta Ordinance Depot, Atlanta Georgia.

A great portion of Donald's service was spent in Europe. He left the States on the S.S. Brazil in October 1944 arriving first in England. He spent some time there then moved on to France, Germany, and Holland. He served in the 15th Army with Company B of the 288th Engineering Company Battalion. According to his discharge papers, while there, he served as a "Tool Room Keeper". He returned to the States in August/September 1945 on the S.S. Victory.

Because he did not have enough points to be discharged from the service when he returned from Europe, Donald was trained in Bomb Disposal and spent some time clearing training grounds of bombs here in the States so that those lands might be returned to civilian use. He was Honorably Discharged April 2, 1946 from Fort Dix, New Jersey.

The Letters and their discovery

Donald Vail wrote regularly to his Mother and Dad from the time he entered the U.S. Army until he was discharged. His mother kept the letters and my sisters and I discovered them in his belongings following his death in 2002. To read these letters sequentially is to read a diary of his experience in the U.S. Army from beginning to end.

The integrity of the letters has been maintained as much as possible by retaining Donald's own misspellings, word omissions and word misusages. By doing so, it reflects his education/learning as a 19 year-old, but also reveals his fatigue and speed with which he was writing his letters. In addition to writing to his Mother and Dad, he was also writing letters to friends, potential love interests, neighbors and other family members while in the service. You will see that he commonly misspells, "Wednesday" as "Wenesday," and "hundred" as "hundered". Again, his original work has been retained to maintain the integrity of his letters.

In life with him, our dad rarely referred to his service in the Army as highlighted in these letters. He would answer questions but reveal little else. This is puzzling in retrospect because so many of the events and occurrences described in his letters essentially reveal defining moments of his life; service to his country in the face of war, the search for love, preparations for a career and so on. In addition, the letters reveal moments of humor and personal tastes which so give a sense of who Donald was.

These letters also reveal prejudices, thoughts, imperfections and more that were never intended to be placed under the scrutiny of a wider audience. Understand them in the context of that time and stage of life of a 19 year-old seeking to serve in a time of national crisis and one just beginning to make his way in the world.

The letters were discovered, as mentioned, after our father Donald's death in 2002. His own father died in 1970 and his mother in 1997. Betty Lou Vail, his wife, died in 2001. Prior to dad's death, we did not know of the letter's existence. Until recently my sisters and I had not read them in their entirety and in sequence.

Also included are letters from family and friends in the Appences at the back of the book. Some are noted in the context of Donald's letters. Some are not.

Donald served his country honorably offering a substantive contribution to the war effort. These letters are shared not because his offering was exceptional compared to any others', but simply for their revelation of a common soldier and man answering the call of duty.

Dates and Places of Donald's War Service

Of his own accord, Donald kept a travel log of the places he went.

June 4, 1943	New Brunswick, New Jersey
June 8, 1943	Fort Dix, New Jersey
June 8-9, 1943	Fort Dix, Pennsylvania, New York, Canada, Michigan to Fort Custer
August 25, 1943	Fort Custer, Indiana, Illinois
August 26, 1943	Iowa, Nebraska, Kansas to POW Camp Concordia, Kansas
September 1943	Fort Hays, Kansas
November 1, 1943	POW Camp
November 28, 1943	POW Camp to Dunellen via Kansas, Nebraska, Iowa, Illinois, Indiana, Ohio, Pennsylvania, New York, New Jersey

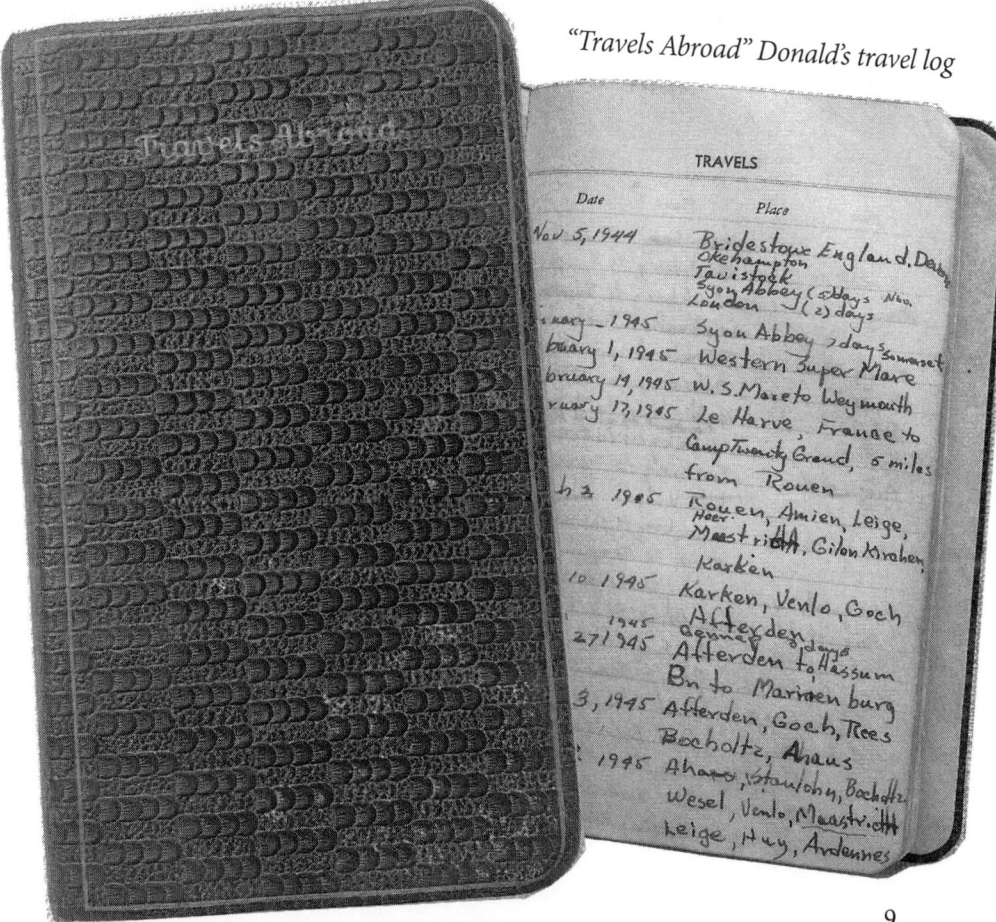

"Travels Abroad" Donald's travel log

December 13, 1943	POW Camp
December 17, 1943	POW Camp to ASTP
December 18, 1943	Grinell, Iowa, Kansas, Nebraska, Iowa
February 1, 1944	Grinell to Illinois, Indiana, Ohio
February 3, 1944	Kentucky to University of Tennessee, Tennessee
March 24, 1944	University of Tennessee to Kentucky, Indiana
March 25, 1944	Camp Atterbury
April 2, 1944	Camp Atturbury to Illinois
April 2, 1944	Missouri to Camp Crowder
April 2, 1944	Camp Crowder to Arkansas, Tennessee, Mississippi, Camp Rucker, Alabama
June 3, 1944	Camp Rucker to Atlanta Ordinance Depot, Georgia
September 4,5, 1944	Atlanta to Camp Rucker
September 2, 1944	Camp Rucker to Georgia, to South Carolina, North Carolina, Virginia, Washington D.C. Maryland, Pennsylvania, New Jersey
October 4, 1944	Return Trip
October 13, 1944	Camp Rucker to Georgia, South Carolina
October 14, 1944	North Carolina, Virginia, Washington D. C. Maryland, Pennsylvania, New Jersey, Camp Shanks, New York
October 20, 1944	Camp Shanks to New Jersey and return
October 21, 1944	Camp Shanks to S.I. *(Staten Island)*
October 22, 1944	Left. N.J. shoreline
November 1, 1944	Irish and Wales Coastline
November 4, 1944	Disembarked at Swansea
November 5, 1944	Bridestowe, England. Devon, Okehampton, Tavistock, Syon Abbey, (5) days, London (2) days
January 1945	Syon Abbey 7 days
February 1, 1945	Western-super-Mare, Somerset
February 14, 1945	Western-super-Mare to Weymouth
February 17, 1945	Le Harve, France to Camp Twenty Grand, 5 miles from Rouen

March 3, 1945	Rouen, Amien, Leige, Maastricht, Gilen\ Kirchen, Karken
March 10, 1945	Karken, Venlo, Goch, Afferden
March 1945	Gennep 3 days
March 27, 1945	Afferden to Hassum, Bn to Marienburg
April 3, 1945	Afferden, Goch, Rees Bocholtz, Ahaus
April 12, 1945	Ahaus, Stadtlohn, Bocholtz Wesel, Venlo, Maastricht, Leige, Huy, Ardennes Luxumborg, Trier Kirchberg
May 1945	Kirchberg to Womrath, Womrath to Pfeddeshein
May 6, 1945	Pfeddershein to Otterberg
June 1945	Otterberg to Pfeddershein
July 1945	Pfeddershein to Melsungen, Frankfurt, Mannheim, Munich, Melsungen to Freising
August 8, 1945	Freising to Frankfort to Bamberg
August	Bamberg to Swinefurt to Mainz to Camp Lucky Strike
August 30, 1945	Lucky Strike to Le Harve
August 31, 1945	Le Harve to U.S.A. via U.S.S. Victory
September 7, 1945	Camp Shanks, New York
September 8, 1945	Ft. Dix, New Jersey
October 25, 1945	Ft. Belvoir, Virginia
November 13, 1945	9800 TSU. Ft. Belvoir, Virginia
November 20, 1945	9301 TSU. Ord School Aberdeen Proving Ground, Maryland
December 1, 1945	Ft. Belvoir, Virginia
January 8, 1946	Ft. Belvoir, Virginia to Atlanta, Georgia
January 1946	Wilmington, North Carolina, Atlanta, Georgia Thomasville and Valdosta, Georgia, Myrtle Beach, South Carolina, St. Petersburg, Florida
February 1946	Wilmington North Carolina

Basic Training

Donald enlists,
gets shipped about
and lands at Ft. Custer, Michigan

June 5, 1943
Fort Dix, New Jersey

Dear Mother and Dad,

Well they keep telling me I'm a soldier now. We got here about two o'clock yesterday and got our first processing. We received mess kits, raincoat, and toilet articles. This took the rest of the afternoon. After supper we learned how to make beds and finally got three aptitude tests. The results were listed on one of the cards during our processing today. On the first general aptitude test (I.Q.) I got a 141 (not bad). Ernie said I needed to 115 to be able to receive engineering training. The next test was the radio receiving aptitude. The only thing you could do was guess on answers so I got an 85 out of a possible 150 the last test was right up my alley. I got a 148 out of 150 on this mechanical aptitude quiz.

Today we got our uniforms and three shots in the arm. We have to wear the fatigue outfits most of the time. As usual I fainted for half a minute after the three shots were in. This afternoon we saw training films except for the excessive heat. The sergeant gave us a lecture on military courtesy for 3/4 of an hour and advised us to go to the movies tonight. The picture is "Mission to Moscow."

I put all the civilian clothes in the mail and you should receive them within several days. From now on everything is "G.I." As soon as I get to permanent station send some clothes hangers as you can't leave clothes around unless you have hangers.

The food here is plentiful, but you need to be hungry to eat it all. The life is pretty good up to now, except that you don't get too much sleep the first night.

You can't visit here nor can I telephone to you. We are now in a twenty-one day quarantine unless we get shipped out first.

It is best not to write while I am here as I will probably be sent out soon. Don't write now.

Love,
Donald

June 6, 1943
Fort Dix, New Jersey

Dear Mother and Dad,

I don't know whether or not this letter will get home at the same time as the letter I wrote last night. I forgot to enclose the receipt for the insurance so I'll send it today. Put the A.S.M.E. pin in the box with the Honor Society pin and the Rensselaer medal.

Today we have quite a bit of time to ourselves. We went to church twice this morning. The first time was an Episcopalian communion. The second was a regular church service with two chaplains leading it. The speaker was the Episcopalian Bishop for New Jersey. He was very interesting, but I really fell asleep as I did not get into the barracks until 11:00, which is taps. When you get up at 5:30 it doesn't give you much sleep.

This afternoon we had to drill for more than an hour. This was not bad, but the drilling was sloppy as we are still a bunch of rookies.

I think I'll take a shower and take a short nap if I can. The fellow in the lower bed has fun by kicking up the springs, so you don't get much of a rest.

The G.I. shoes feel pretty good so far and I hope they still will. Buy a shaving brush and add it to the stuff to be sent to the next camp.

Love,
Donald

June 8, 1943
Fort Custer, Michigan

Dear Mother and Dad,

We were just beginning our trip to an unknown destination. We started out from our barracks about 3:00 and left Fort Dix about 4:20 it is now 7:00 and we're just outside of Philadelphia heading west. The station just passed was Bryn Mawr. This is been a slow ride as we seem to stop every 5 minutes for 10 or more minutes. Passed Villanova now, the first Lieutenant talked to us for a while and said that we would not be told where we are going as possible sabotage might occur if we sent out letters or phones calls. We have not had our 4:30 mess yet but the call will probably come soon. The Negro cooks are in the next car and if the car door is open we get a car full of smoke from the wood fire. Tonight we eat the mess from our paper plates and cups, but the lieutenant threatened to make us eat the next meal from our mess kits if any plates are thrown from windows.

This looks like a long trip for us as the Lieutenant said we would probably shave on the train. We have stopped again to release or change one of the steam engines, I think. Any smudges on the paper come from the coal dust. We have started again with new engines.

There are about fifty of us in this car but only one or two from Dunnellen. From the looks of this outfit I say we were headed for an infantry division or perhaps the engineers, but the infantry is more probable. Joey is riding the same train but in a different section of it. This means that the rear cars will be shunted off for some other destination.

We're now passing Frazer some stop up in the mountains and no one seems to be sure but the general direction is still west. I spent some time reading the soldiers handbook before I decide to begin this letter, which probably won't be finished until we hit the new station.

I'm riding with a fellow named Eddie Rowe from near Boonton. We were bunking in adjacent beds at Fort Dix. He hopes to get in the ski troops after he finishes basic training. He's twenty-two, married, and wants to get ahead in this army. We both ought to get some where with this crew as a lot of them are Jews or foreigners with quite a few of them from Brooklyn.

It is 7:30 and we are all hungry. The last town we passed was Downing Town. The scenery is pretty with green fields and low mountains.

It is now 9:50 and we have just finished mess. The meal was good, but sloppy. We had Virginia ham, pineapple, potatoes, and salad. The train is moving at a rapid rate and cans of water and coffee were spilling all over the mess car floor. The last city we stopped at was Harrisburg where Union News lost some money. They sold us cheap sandwiches and had to buy them back after the Lieutenant kicked. It is dark so we can't tell where we are and I believe the next stop is Akron.

There are only 5 cars left, so Joey must have been shipped South as they were dropped at North Philadelphia. Let me know where he was sent as I have no way of knowing.
This afternoon we were drilled by an AUS (wounded and returned from Africa) Master Sergeant. He was excellent and we were even willing to stay for more as it was fun.
Some of the fellows are writing, others are sleeping, and some are playing poker and Knock rummy. I think I'll try to sleep in a little while.

I had my picture taken at Fort Dix in the fatigue suit. The hat makes me look like a member of a Georgia chain gang, I know, but I'll send the shot to you anyway. We have been traveling across country but we just passed thru some town. The railroad passes along the main street. The boys wanted to stop for a beer.

We have passed thru some steel mill town, but too fast to read the signs. We had to wear our sun tans and they are dirty already. This means I'll have to wash them when we get there. I hope we won't do any work tomorrow as I'll be dead tired. A crap game is going on in the back of the car and Rowie just got a deck of cards to play Rummy. (Lost 15 cents).

June 9th

What a night!! I got about 4 hours sleep. We have been riding all over the country. I woke up and found that we were in Buffalo at 5:30. We have stopped now for supplies before we start again. Perhaps we are going to Fort Niagara or an on a boat. Who knows?

About 11:15 after passing Harrisburg by 100 miles repass a very bad wreck on the Pennsylvania R. R. A number of hopper cars were derailed, as was the engine. Has it been reported in the papers? During the night it rained and we could not see where we were going except for reports that we were still in Pennsylvania or New York. It is 6:15 and we're on the move. The sun is up so it won't be so bad when we move in.

We are now crossing the Niagagra River and can see several freighters. There is also a large canal and Lake Erie in sight. All the sailor are up at the Coast Guard station. Canada is just across a long, steel, arch bridge. The water in that river is really running rapidly. On the siding is a circus which reminds me of the Ringling Bros. train we saw in Philly.

The train is now crossing into Canada our destination is again unknown. This is the St. Lawrence River. Canada at 6:50. The weather is some what cooler but the scenery is much the same.

This is really something. Five days in the Army and we are seeing the world. There is no telling where we headed for. Perhaps I'll be able to continue this letter for another day. The houses are few and far between with most of the land pastoral with trees along the boarders. The farms grow wheat, hay, & alfalfa. The farms are all irrigated. At 8:00 we passed a Canadian airfield and saw several planes in the air.

We have had mess and are going to play cards for a while. Send a straight deck out to me as there is a dollar tax on the street deck.

Sometime ago we passed thru Tillsonburgh. About 8:00 we stopped at Saint Thomas, Ontario which is 115 miles from Niagagra Falls and 112 miles from Detroit. It is now 10:00 and scenery is still the same.

At 10:35 we can see Detroit in the distance and must ride through a mile long tunnel under the Susquehanna River before we hit the states again. It won't seem bad to see towns and cities after seeing the continuous farms in Canada. Everyone is restless and tired of sitting for eighteen hours. The engine is being replaced so we can expect another ride with a new one for an hour and a half or two hours. The engines have been replaced about eight or nine times. The RCAF has quite a few flying fields along the line and it seems like they are covering our trip with their flights. I sold some of the Philip Morris the Raoul gave me, as some of the fellows were out of them. This stop was Winsor. I can see a large suspension bridge in the distance. We are about to enter the tunnel. Half the lights are out in the car as they were loosened while we slept and finally they dropped nearly hitting several fellows.

We stayed in the tunnel about 5 minutes. We're home again! We're using an electric engine in place of the dirty steam engines. We getting more ice that means another meal on the train.

We left the station at 11:25 and passed the Ford River Rouge Plant, tabernacle, and housing project soon after that. The engineer buildings are neat and well designed. The change in scenery is very apparent all the buildings and houses are modern. There are a number of housing projects in the suburban area.

We get about 1 1/2 to 2 hours more riding. My new address is in Michigan, but we don't know where. The address will be on the envelope. I'll write soon.

Love,
Donald

P. S. I might as well continue this letter before I take a shower. We arrived after 20 hours at Fort Custer and marched to our barracks. You'd never guess but I am in the MP's. The address is 427MPEG Co. Fort Custer, Mich. This outfit will patrol all different types of areas, Prisoners of War and the like.
Send hangers, socks (white and suntans), and Joe Houska's address which is in the top drawer of the cabinet. Send any mail or new addresses of Ernie and Joey.   Don

June 9, 1943
Fort Custer, Michigan

Dear Mother

The address on the letter that I put in the mail was incorrect. The correct number is 474 MPEG Co. The letters stand for Military Police Escort Guard Company. The officers were brought in here two weeks ago, with some men who have had basic training. This seems like a good outfit as the non-com officers are all nice people, all with American sounding names. This is going to be a tough outfit to go thru with. We start training tomorrow on this 6 to 9 week course. They are really going to rush it, so I won't have much time to write for a while.

There is a clothing check going on as I write this note. I hope everything is all right. Let me know how things are at home.

Love,
Donald

June 13, 1943
Fort Custer, Mich

Dear Mother and Dad,

Yesterday we were assigned to a different unit in the MPEG's. This was caused by the decision of some officer who thought it better to fill up the 6th Battalion by Monday rather than waiting until Tuesday by which time the 5th would have been filled. Our new company is the 480 MPEG. Co. and should be just as good as the other that we have just left. The list of things that we will do next week has been posted and we will not have a minute of rest during the day. Everything will run according to the clock so that no time will be wasted.

Today is Sunday and we did not have to get up until 7:45 and mess was at 8:00. There is another check on our G.I. clothing and other equipment that has been issued to us. This is about the fourth time in a week. Friday after we got another typhoid shot (it did not knock me out), we were issued gas mask, MP club, MP armband, and our pack equipment. At night we had to learn how to pack the light and regular pack.

We have been learning our General Orders which are the army Bylaws. You have to know these orders before you can get a pass to leave the post. I know most of them now, but we can not leave until our two week quarantine period is finished. Battle Creek is six miles from here and there is the small town of Augusta at a distance of two and half miles.

There are about four of us in a sort of cliche. Besides Ed Rowe who I rode with on the train there is Brant Taylor from Lincoln Park, N.J. up near Caldwell. He is nineteen and only a few days older than myself. He went to college in Ohio and had some engineering there. He is a nice fellow and a good pal. The third fellow is Leo Samuels from Center Street, Dunellen. Leo lived in Rhule's house the other side of Fairview Ave. He is interested in mechanics and we get along together. There is the possibility that we may be able to get into the motor pool of this Battalion and get a rating. Stripes will be given out as the training progresses and there are only a few non-coms to run against us.

I have not received anything that you may have sent me but if you have included any of the articles I will mention forget about them. I sent the laundry out Wenesday and am having to buy more supplies to last me. I will always be able to use more towels (Bath and linen hand), Wash clothes, socks (white wool sweat and cotton suntans), and under-shirts and shorts. You had better send more of the writing paper, later I'll buy writing paper here that has our insignia, crossed horse pistols, on it.

Even though it is Sunday we have to wash down our barracks. The barracks have not been used for a period of time. We are beginning to believe that MPEG stands for Mop Pail and Elbow Grease. The boys are started a half hour early after our dinner. We had an excellent chicken Frigazee for dinner.

This afternoon we washed barracks. We were given passes but I don't think that I'll use mine as there is enough to do here and I don't drink beer. It takes too long to get back I have heard. We won't get any more passes for two weeks.

The only thing that takes much money here is for clothes and odds and ends. Ice cream is $.15 a pint and everything is very cheap. If you can spare about $10 I'll have my picture taken in the PX. A good set will cost about $6.

We will probably go to a show or play ping pong in a day room across the street.

I don't know how much time I'll have to write from tomorrow on but I'll try to write as often as possible.

Love,
Don

Father's Day card

Text on card: *front:* "A wish for you on Father's Day"

  inside: "Wishing you health, good fortune too,
       The joy of your wishes, all come true,
       With each day always a day of cheer,
       Each year a happy and lucky year.
       Thinking of you on Father's Day.
       Wishing you joy along life's way.
       Hoping new interests and success
       May add to your daily happiness.
          (signed) Don

(note on back of card)

June 17, 1943
Fort Custer Mich.

Dear Mother and Dad,

    We began our basic Monday and we are working like Dogs from 8 AM until 5 PM in the field and theater. At nights we wash barrack for a while. Yesterday we had our first casualty as one of the Jewish fellows who was always putting on an act was hurt while we were playing a tagging game. We have not heard how he is as yet. Ed Rowe was chasing him when he fell. Friday we will go on a four mile hike, but our barracks are a mile from the training field, and we walk this several times a day, so we won't feel the hike too much. It is hard to find time to write, but I'll attempt to write a letter on Sunday. The life here is swell and it is impossible to transfer or get a furlough.

    Love,
    Don

Pvt. Donald Vail ASN 32923472 480 MPEG Co.
Fort Custer Mich.

June 20, 1943
Fort Custer, Mich

Dear Mother and Dad,

It is almost 12:30 when we eat but I decided to begin writing you a letter. I'm in the day room of the Provost Marshall Company which is across the street from our barracks. Most of the fellows are writing letters, but a few are playing cards. There is also a radio, a ping pong table, and a coke machine here so it is not so bad.

Our first week of our nine week maximum of training is at an end and it certainly has been tough. During the week we have had lectures from officers and non-commissioned officers. These lectures have covered military courtesy, care of equipment, and identification of airplanes and tanks. Every day we have seen moving pictures in one of the theaters. We have seen so many that even if we had time we would not want to go to a picture at night. Every night we've had to pack equipment or wash the barracks. We have finally finished washing the barracks today, I hope. I also hope that they won't decide to move our company nearer the training field or the balance of our battalion.

Friday afternoon we went on a four mile hike with full pack and steel helmets. I was glad when it was finished as were the other fellows. As yet I have not gotten any blisters, but I have a rash on my feet caused by the heat. The weather here is perfect as it does not get too hot and the nights are cool so that we sleep with one woolen G.I. Blanket over us. Monday night we will go on another four mile hike, but this time we will carry our rifles which were issued Saturday. We'll again be glad to take a shower and fall in bed. All next week we probably will be in the field until late and won't get supper until 8:30. This will be another tough week but we will be able to get passes again at the end of the week.

As yet that package that you said you mailed has not arrived. I don't know what happened to it unless you didn't mail it until later in the week. Buy a pair of swimming trunks if you can and send it out to me. They have opened a large lake on the camp area for swimming. I can buy anything here that I need, but we won't be paid until the first of the month.

The meals here are generally good but Friday everyone was griping because the food was slight and not well liked. We had ham, mashed potatoes, peas and carrots, chopped green salad, a type of gravy with raisins, and ice cream for our Sunday Dinner. There were plenty of seconds and I could hardly walk away from the table.

Drop me a line a let me know how things are going.

Love,
Don

June 27, 1943
Fort Custer, Mich

Dear Mother and Dad,

All of my mail was finally straightened out by Friday as I received your first package on Thursday and the one that you mailed June 19th on Tuesday or Wenesday. Thanks for everything that you mailed to me. I have plenty of socks and towels, but I'll have to buy some more underwear at the PX. The laundry did not pick up the wash this week, so we will have to go two weeks with out a really clean wash. It also means that I'll have to wash my fatigues and some of the other web gear this morning.

About two-thirds of the fellows in the barracks, went out on passes last night and as yet only a few have returned. One or two of the fellows were angry because they could not go to Detroit, because of the race riots they are having there. You probably know more about them than I do as I have not been able to read a paper this week. I now that one of M.P. regiments was sent there as well as one or two M.P.E.G. Companies. I have heard that some of the southern fellows in our company were wishing that they might go.

Instead of taking a pass for Kalamazoo (a truck convoy will take you & return you) Brant and I decided to hang around camp. Sergeant Piette (from Racine, Wis.) gave us tickets to a dance at the Field House. The C.O. said that there were going to be 2000 girls there but a more correct estimate was 350 as against a 1000 soldiers. The two bands from two sections of the different M.P. outfits here put out some good music so the dance was not so bad.

This pass week was tough and I'm still wondering how I got thru it and I still cannot remember what happened most of the time. All I can remember of Monday i that we came in off the field at 5:00 after an exceptionally hot day as three or four fellows were felled with heat exhaustion. After 5:00 we packed the full pack and started on a night hike at 8:30 as dark clouds and the wind rose. After we had gone a half mile, we put on our raincoats and returned in the barracks, finally the hike again started at 9.30 in a light rain after much trouble and indecision. We finally got back about 11:00 and I was dog tired after plodding thru the muddy roads.

They gave us coffee and sandwich and we had to clean our rifle so we finally got to bed at 12:30. Tuesday afternoon we had to drill in the heat for Retreat Parade that night. As usual the 480th was the last on the Parade Grounds for which I was glad as my feet were about worn off. Thursday afternoon we went on the same hike but this time everything was sandy and it was just as bad as Monday night. After this we had to walk another mile with full pack to the .22 rifle range where I could just about lift the rifle. Wenesday night we were in the field until 8:00 and Thursday it was 7:30. Friday we went into the gas chamber as described in the book that I'll mail to you in the same mail but it you won't get until several days later.

Saturday was easy on us as all we did besides having a 25 question quiz and equipment and rifle inspection was to run the obstacle course in the afternoon. The toughest part of this was crawling under the barbed wire; it seemed as if it took me two hours to get thru it.

I think I'll close now as I have more letters to write as everyone dropped me a line this week. I got letters from Ernie, El, Ed Pyatt, Bud, Uncle Roy, Claire and Marion.

Write when you can.

Love,
Don

July 4, 1943
Fort Custer, Mich.

Dear Mother and Dad,

What a way I sent a July 4th. For the second time this week, I had K.P. It seems that Monday our company had Guard Duty around the Post during the night. As I was in the V's my name did not come up but I had to stay on the Alert Platoon. On this Platoon you have to be ready to answer any call, and are awaken twice during the night to report. You also sleep in your clothes so I did have any clothes to have my picture taken in this week. As a result of most of the fellows being on Guard I had to do K.P. Tuesday. Wenesday the old tough First Sergeant was replaced by one of the corporals (quite a rise for him). The other sergeant had the list mixed up so my name again came up for K.P. on Sunday. Sunday was fairly easy as most of the fellows were out on weekend passes so that there weren't so many dishes or pans to wash & clean. I was sick of doing pans on Tuesday though.

This week was not as tough on us physically. I guess we're beginning to get use to it by now. The only hard part is that are not enough hours in the day to do everything that the army wants done. Saturday is about the only easy day except that there is inspection and quiz on the material covered during the week. This week we had a quiz on marksmanship positions which I passed satisfactorily. I was caught on inspection though as the Lieutenant found dirt in the chamber of the rifle, so I'll get some extra duty this week for several hours. I was not the only one caught as over 50% of section had the same dirty crack. The Lieutenant must have had a bad night I guess.

We went over the obstacle course twice this week and each time it gets a little easier. We were scheduled for two five mile marches but I did not have to go on the first because of the guard duty. The second was very easy as it was on a clear cool night and I did not mind the walking at all.

Several days have been so cool this week that I was wearing the woolen undershirt. One morning, the temperature was 49°F in our barracks. The weather is again normal today.

Your package arrived yesterday and thanks again for everything. The only thing that I need is the pair of wooden sandals if you can buy them.

I don't know how much time I'll have to write as next week are supposed to go out on the range and shoot our rifles for records. You need a 132 out of 200 points to qualify and if you don't qualify you have to make it up on a Sunday or take the training over. Thursday we shot the .22 again, and, I did all right there, and I hope can so the same with the regular rifle. When we go on the range we will eat early in the morning, about 4 or 5 o'clock eat dinner and supper off of mess kits in the field and return to the barracks about nine o'clock. We have been told that this training will ease up after the range shooting is passed. I certainly hope so.

Saturday, I was planning to go to Kalamazoo on the truck convoy but I could get a pass because of the K.P. Brant Taylor and Ed Rowe went anyway. I hope that we will get weekend passes again within several weeks although the officers have said that we may not get passes for the next three weeks.

Let me know how things are going on in Dunellen. That is all for a while.

Love,
Don

July 11, 1943
Fort Custer, Mich

Dear Mother and Dad,

Well another week has gone by and as usual I am wondering how we were able to complete it without the third section losing any more men. We began with about 32 men but about 10 have been unable to stand the pace because of some physical defect. Most of these have been the older men.

The first man to receive a PFC rating since coming into the company was a fellow named, Jim Malone. He reminds me of Ted Wann quite a bit as he is tall, has gray hair, and has the same general appearance. He and Brant Taylor have been appointed our acting corporals and both will probably get the rating in a week or two. I hope I am able to get a P.F.C. before this training is completed, but then who knows.

As usual we have been working day and night all this week. One night we went on another march up and down the hills around this post. It was warm but I am glad it does not get as hot as it does in Alabama or Texas where Ernie and Bud are. I received letters from both in the last couple of days. Bud told me of a party that he went to on one weekend. He must be hitting the millionaire class from the size of party and property owned by the girl he went with. As for me I have yet to get a pass.

Again this week no passes were issued and we are going to fire the Enfield rifle on the range on Monday, Tuesday, and Wenesday for record. I need a 134 out of a possible 200 to qualify, which is the army term for making the score. To make sure we did not leave camp (AWOL) we had to do guard duty last night. This time I had to walk the post with two hours on and four off. As usual with my luck I drew the hardest relief. The third relief work from 22:00 (10:00) to midnight and from 4:00 to 6:00 AM. This is not too easy on a Saturday night as there are soldiers coming in at all hours and everyone must be challenged begin 11:00 and 6:00. It rained intermittently during the night to add to our difficulties and one relief had to take their post in a downpour.

I hope I am able to have that picture taken soon. It is either a case of not having the time or I don't have a clean set of sun tans. The latter is the case today after last night.

Yesterday was our first payday (I got $40.00). As the boys don't have any place to go to spend their money they are gamboling quite a bit. A couple of hundered of dollars changed hands in the guard house last night and a crap game has been going on all morning. Before yesterday Brant, Ed, and I played poker for pennies but we able to play for nickels now.

It has started raining today and it will probably be a dreary day from our stand point. I hope the training will easy up after this next week but I will write again on next Sunday.

Love,
Don

P.S. I got the newspapers and crackers, but I should say crumbs not crackers. I also got a letter from Aunt Ruth and a card from Lou Lofetia this week. D.

July 18, 1943
Fort Custer, Mich

Dear Mother and Dad,

Another week has been completed and I am still sleepy as an after affect. I have not been able to get a full eight sleep for the past week and it is doubtful as to how much sleep we will get this week. The night of guard duty I had three hours, & Sunday night about five as we got up a three in the morning to go out on the range to shoot. Monday and Tuesday we had four or five hours before getting up. Wenesday night there were only four hours sleep as I drew K.P. again for Thursday. The hours were long that day from five to twelve, midnight, that night as we had to work until the fellows returned from a night hike. Saturday we again got up early to shoot on the .22 range at moving targets. This was supposed to be practice for shooting at airplanes.

Last night I was lucky as I got a pass by the skin of my teeth. The first order that we got was that all men who failed to qualify with a rifle were to be restricted to clean rifles, but Lieutenant Broyles, our company command finally got us passes with the understanding that we had to be in camp as eight this morning to clean the rifles. At least this was a good break for us. There were thirty four of us in the company who failed to qualify including Brant and myself. I hit a 110 in the preliminary firing, but I could not hit any thing during the record firing so I ended up with a 90. This probably won't make much difference as I was assigned a shot gun so that I could hit something perhaps.

Last night, we went to Battle Creek which is not such a bad town. We went shopping for a while, buying different things that we needed. Brant, Bob Sherer, and I finally decided to go skating after we found a rink. After skating we went to a Chinese restaurant and ate Chow Mein and this really hit the spot.

I'll close now with prospects for another tough week in sight.

Love,
Donald

P.S. We get better and more food since Friday when everyone complained to the CO about the mess and the food.

July 25, 1943
Fort Custer, Mich.

Dear Mother and Dad,

Our sixth week was completed yesterday with more range firing. This time it was the carbine which is a light weapon used in place of the pistol or revolver as it has a greater accuracy and range. I qualified in the records with an 85 out of a hundred but this isn't a too accurate score. Our own men were scoring our targets so naturally a few points were added in the pits by scoring previous bullet holes or other slight errors in marking. The coaches were also using what is known as the thirty calibre pencils to improve low scores. I still probably had a fairly good score as my sights were on the bull's eyes yesterday. The day before we had a few shots with the Thompson sub machine gun which is another handy weapon to have in case of an arguement. That gun surely can spray the bullets around. Wenesday we had a few shots with the shot gun. It isn't necessary to aim this shot gun, all you do is to pull the trigger and the chances are that the shot will spray your target.

We will have completed our range firing after we fire the Enfield for record again, the pistol, and the machine gun. To-morrow we get up at three o'clock to fire the Enfield rifle and I have got to qualify or else, but I think I'll be able to do it with out too much trouble even without the .30 calibre pencil. Wenesday we fire the pistol by we have not had any experience or instruction with this weapon so we only get a few practice shots are the target just to say that we have fired it.

Last Tuesday I have my first taste of guarding prisoners or chasing prisoners as the army calls it. I had to take four prisoners from the stockade out of a work detail of bailing paper. We were given live ammunition for the rifle for any trouble that might be started, but the fellows I had were fellows that had gone A.W.O.L. and were serving light sentences so they did not start any trouble for me. The bad part was that I could not sit down until the prisoners were returned to the stockade.

I am glad to hear that Una is happily married and that the wedding was a success. How are the rest of things in Dunellen and Plainfield? The weather is warm but not hot as it probably is home. Write soon.

Love,
Don

P.S. Here is a book we got at Fort Custer.

August 1, 1943
Fort Custer, Mich.

Dear Mother and Dad,

The beginning of another month and the time sure has flown since I was home last. After you finish one week it seems like a day or so, but it is hard to recall what happened during the week there has been so much in it. I finally qualified with the rifle this week. My final record score was 155 out of 200 which makes me a marksman. The previous day I had shot a 166 in preliminary firing but I could not equal it on Tuesday. If I had a score of 168 or better I would've been a sharpshooter; over 178 is an expert. Wenesday we spent a day out on the range waiting for a chance to fire the pistol and revolver for fifteen minutes. It seems that the 480th gets to police up every range after firing as we are always the last to do anything, but always the first to arrive. This sure does burn us up at times.

Don't every get the idea that this army is completely mechanized for the M.P. to use their feet more than any other mode of transportation. Friday we did a eight mile forced march during the day. It was a good thing that a fair breeze was blowing as this dried our sweat and made marching over the hills much easier. Tomorrow we are going to do ten miles and I hope that the stiff breeze that is blowing today will continue.

Last night Brant and I got passes for Kalamazoo where we spent more money on eating then anything else. As a town it is a little larger than Plainfield with more hotels, taverns, and movie theaters. We saw a show and returned on a "Greyhound" with 60 or 70 other soldiers.

I hope the pictures arrived all right. These were to have been mailed on Friday by the photographer here at camp. The fellows thought they (the pictures) came out fairly good.

We sure are getting some good meals now as the mess sergeants of the two companies eating in our mess hall were stripped of their rank for inefficiency. Last night's and our to-day's dinner were probably the two best meals that I have had in the Army.

Brant's and my pass were limited to two o'clock this afternoon as we were given a fluff detail. About five or six of us were assigned to go to a picknic at Eagle Lake with some gals brought in from one of the towns near here. At least I'll be able to use the swimming trunks for the first time since I have been here.

I was glad to hear that Ed called to see you. It would be nice to see that soldier again.

How do you like cooking now after the session with the string beans. Prices must be high if peaches at $5.00 a baskets. How are other things now.

The next letter may be written from a tent here in camp, but I'll still write.

Love,
Donald

Sunday, August 8
Fort Custer, Mich.

Dear Mother and Dad,

Another Sunday is here and things are still as busy as ever. Tonight everyone is preparing to move out in the morning to the bivouac area.* It sure is a mad house around here but there is one consolation it will be the last Sunday in Fort Custer. This morning I did K.P. for a couple of hours for a fellow for two bucks as I was short of money. The reason for this as that I am going to enclose a money order for twenty-five dollars.

Tonight I have to do some special guard duty. I have a relief from twelve to two of guarding a few loaded trucks. I had only one full night's sleep last week and probably I won't get one this week. We had regular guard duty Tuesday night. Friday I had to coach on the machine gun range. It took a while to get use to the noise but finally I caught two hours sleep in back of the range.

We were informed of recommendation for promotions today. I am up for a P.F.C. rating. Brant is also due for the same while Ed Rowe is due for corporal's stripes. If we get them you can really say that we earned those stripes.

I am going to enclose a poem written by Ed Rowe's father and it sound pretty good to me. It could be very appropriate if we go west. The serge was in Arizona and he say we will just "love" the west if we go that way, but you must put the proper emphasis on that word.

I'll close now as I want to get a couple of hours of sleep before I go out.

Love,
Don

August 9, 1943
Fort Custer, Mich.

Dear Mother and Dad,

We left our comfortable barracks early this morning but we have had a fairly easy day so far today. Everyone had to march about two and a half miles with full field pack to large field where we are bivouacked. It was hard on a lot of fellows who are waiting transfer to limited service and thus to discharge from the army. About five or six left last Saturday and probably ten or more will be discharged sooner or later. We got here about eight o'clock and spent the balance of the morning pitching our tents three or four times.

This afternoon, all we had to due was go on a swimming detail. We walked five or six miles before we located the creek where we were to swim. I was really tired all day as I only had four hours sleep between the two reliefs that I had last night. The guard duty was easy as there was no one to challenge.

Tonight, we are due for a ten mile hike which should be easy as we are only wearing gas mask, steel helmet, light Combat pack, and carring my shotgun. Last Monday afternoon, a fairly warm day, we did ten miles, but with a heavy pack and that can tire you out in a short time.

Thursday night we had a six miler with a tear gas attack. That really is not any fun, especially if you get a shot of that gas. I don't think I'll wear glasses tonight as the mask will leak wear the rims come back to my ears.

I forgot to enclose that money order, so I'll make sure that it is in this one. I hope that you are not still staying with Mrs. Frazee, can't she get some one else?

My next letter will give my new address. I hope we go East; a group ten companies who left here over the weekend went to Dix and Camp Upton, as rumor has it.

Love,
Donald

MPEG

Military Police Escort Guard

Prisoner of War Camp, Concordia, Kansas
and the Agricultural Experiment Station,
Ft. Hays State College in Hays, Kansas

Monday, August 16, 1943
Prisoners of War Camp, Concordia, Kansas

Dear Mother and Dad,

Well here I am a P.F.C. and deep in heart of Kansas. I was notified last Wenesday that I had gotten my first stripe. There was some kind of a mixup on this deal as some of the fellows who were mentioned for a stripe and really deserved them failed to get them. Brant can be included in this classification. There will be some more stripes given out soon so some of this may be corrected.

After we finished up out on bivouac area we returned to the barracks and prepared to move to a new camp. Rumor had it that we were going to nearly every state in the union but Friday we got a hot tip that we were going to guard prisoners at Concordia, Kansas. Saturday we were up early and got set to leave for the seven o'clock train. We let with four other companies but they were headed for a camp in Illinois and Oklahoma.

Last week we got a new commanding officer, First Lieutenant Ball. He has been in the army for 28 years and saw five battles in the last war. He is really a swell guy from what we have seen of him so far. Lt. Broyles is now second in command.

Friday, we had a fairly good first sergeant but Saturday we lacked him as he probably went A.W.O.L., as far as we know now. Sergeant Piette is acting First Sergeant and I hope that gets all those stripes as he is a swell guy.

We saw the last of Fort Custer at 7:30 AM. In one way were glad as we had to work like dogs on a minimum of sleep. The things that will miss of Michigan are the cities and large town and the scenery of hills and trees. We went west through Kalamazoo to Niles and then into Indiana. We skirted around the bottom of Lake Michigan, but I caught some sleep until we got to Chicago, Ill. about eleven o'clock. We spent about three hours horsing around Chicago. We moved around all the track and switched cars around for the rest of the time.

During the afternoon we crossed Illinois and we began seeing nothing but plains covered with corn and wheat.

After supper we crossed the Mississippi River at a point were it was fairly narrow. We went into Iowa and more plains and fewer hills. We played rummy for several hours to spend the time. I also read a book for several hours until the lights out at 10:30. I slept well on the train and awoke at 6:20 when we were a little past Lincoln, Neb. We poked along a single track railroad all morning until we got to Wymore, Neb. At this small junction of two railroads we saw our first Nazis. They were on a prison train heading for our camp. They seemed to be a bunch of young boys sprinkled with some older men. They were from the African campaign as they had on suntan shorts and caps of a style similar to the French Foreign Legion hat.

During the morning, we hit Kansas which is a hot and dry state. Everything was dried out and the clay was all caked and cracked. We arrived in Concordia at 12:30 and were driven to our new home in truck. Concordia seems to be larger than most of the towns in Kansas, but it going to be a lot deader than Michigan or Jersey.

This is a new camp and is just beginning to be filled up. There will be four MPEG companies guarding several thousand Germany prisoners of war. The life here will be very easy on us as our company will do guard for 24 hours about every third day. The balance of the time we will probably get some light duties but not to many of these. The only thing we have to worry about is not letting any of the prisoners escape. The camp is on a plain and you can see for miles in any direction so you can spot any one. We will get class A passes which will let us go town from five at night until five in the morning every night unless we have duty.

I close now as the mail is supposed to leave now. Write soon.

Love,
Donald

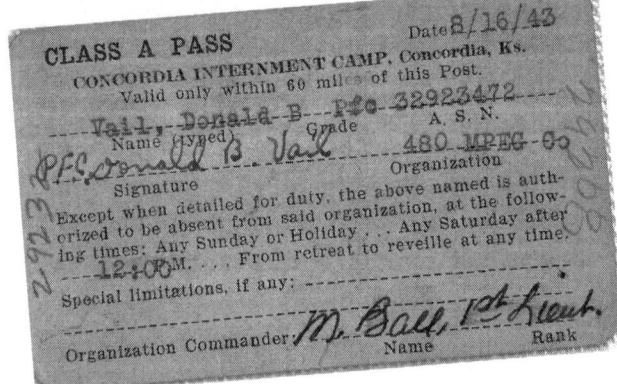

Monday, August 23
Concordia, Kansas

Dear Mother and Dad,

Your letter arrived today and I thought I might as well answer it while I have the time. Summer has returned to Kansas for the temperature has risen to about 110 to 120° in the sun and a little less (108) in the shade. The only thing that keeps us from feeling it too much is that the humidity is low. The climate is very dry, so in one or more respects that is good as we don't have to worry about rust on our rifles (correct spelling) and shot guns.

Tonight, we go on guard duty again and I am on the second relief which is from 9 to 1 at night and the same hours tomorrow morning. This is probably the hardest relief as we don't get very much sleep as they awaken you all time for meals. Friday I had the first relief so I had enough sleep. Tonight I have a hard post as I have to walk around a house inside the compound where German prisoners in solitary are confined. When you are inside of the compounds the only weapon you carry is the billey, so most of your protection comes from the tower guards who are well armed. Friday I was stationed at the entrance of the hospital which is the easiest post as you can sit down every once in a while.

Last Thursday we were chasing prisoners. This consists of taking them out to different places where they are supposed to work. Three prisoners are assigned to each guard so we have to keep on the ball at all times. It is a serious offense to be caught sleeping or being slacks in this company. One of the fellows in our section was seen by a private and the Colonel eating a couple of spoonfuls of ice cream and has since been confined to the barracks awaiting court marshal. I hope nothing serious occurs. He was guarding our AWOL's but it was still enough to be punished. The other companies are slacker than our 480 therefore 480 is not too well liked as we are too GI to suit them.

Can you buy a pair of good sun glasses that will fit over my glasses? The sun certainly can give you a headache after a few hours. If enough fellows buy pith helmets, we will be able to wear them on duty. These helmets make us look like African big game hunters. I'll try to have several pictures taken as there is a good supply of cameras available now.

Concordia isn't too bad a town considering its size. Yesterday they dedicated the honor roll of soldiers and 480 supplied thirty soldiers to make it military. Brant had to lower the flag while the national anthem was played by the Fort Riley cavalry band. I was unable to see it as I had another session in the mess hall as a K.P. Last night I went to hear the Band concert which was excellent. The night before about ten of us went swimming in town in the pool which really was good.

I'm going to take a shower and get dressed before I continue the letter. 480th is back on guard again and I'll finish from the guard house.

The poem that you wrote was good and also appropriate. Brant sends his thanks but I did not have a chance to give Ed his copy. Brant finally got his P.F.C. stripe and Ed got his Corporal stripes. As things stand now, all ratings are issued but there are always stripes changing hands.

I remember hearing the name De Young several times while we were in Dix but I don't remember seeing him at Custer. In case you have not heard 471 and 476 went to Illinois. There are just 40 miles between this camp and Chicago and Racine, Wis. This would have been a swell camp for us, but 480 is an eight ball outfit and always will be. Two other companies went to Oklahoma. This camp is about a day and a half's travel from home. The other two companies are beginning to get ten day furloughs but some of them don't start until December. Furloughs are given in alphabetical order beginning with the lowest rank. This means, I ought to get a furlough about Christmas or later. Oh well, sooner or later!

Send out another dozen hangers if you can get them as we don't have foot lockers. Thanks for newspaper which I got last week. Write when you get time.

Love,
Donald

Sunday, August 29
Concordia, Kansas

Dear Mother and Dad,

Well, here is another Sunday, and it is still hot in Kansas although the nights and mornings are cool enough to be comfortable. We finally got news about furloughs as the list was posted today. The first furloughs begin Wenesday September 1st but the first ones aren't too welcome as everyone is broke and we don't get paid until the tenth as we were traveling when the payroll was supposed to have been made. The men with the longest service in the army are going first and then it goes alphabetically with the majority of the company that came in on the shipment to Custer. With this arrangement, my name is on the next to the last list of men leaving on furloughs.

We are to be given ten days off plus two days traveling time. The date mine is to begin is December 14th while it will end on the 26th. I hope some kind of arrangement will be made so that we will get an extra day so we won't have to leave on Christmas day. With good connections the trip from here to home should take about thirty six hours. The ticket will cost between forty to fifty dollar round trip so someone of us had better start saving some money. The only thing wrong with preparing for this is that we probably won't be stationed at this post in December. I still hope I'll get a furlough for this date even though it is a long time off.

All this week we have been doing routine of chasing prisoners and guard mount. For the last two times I have had to guard a solitary confinement guard house for Germans inside of the compound. On this post I carry a pistol as the Nazi in there attempted to knife a guard one day. Oh well it is all in a day's work.

Another five hundred prisoners were brought here Tuesday night and four hundered came in this morning. This only makes more men for us to chase but only adds a couple of names to the guard roster. There will probably be another shipment before the camp is filled to capacity.

I got the package that you sent and thanks a lot. It looks like I'll have to smoke my pipe more often now with all that tobacco. Brant is going to buy another pipe to help me out. Incidentally Brant is to get his furlough the same time that I get mine so we ought to have a good time while or when we get it. Time passes a lot faster if you have some one to talk to or play cards with when you are on the train.

I'll close now as we have to prepare for guard again to-night. Write when you get a chance.

Love,
Donald

P.S. How much civilian insurance have I? They want to know out here.

Matchbook cover, Concordia, Kansas

Sunday, Sept. 5, 1943
Prisoners of War Camp
Concordia, Kan.

Dear Mother and Dad,

We just came off guard in which we began shooting at the Germans. They are coming too close to the fences, so we were given strict orders to shoot on any occasion. On September 1st we were on guard when they were celebrating the beginning of the fifth year of war. The officers all formed into columns and marched to a large area in the center of the officers compound. A group of about 75 officers sang of the Nazi theme songs a cappella. That is one thing these Nazis can do. The harmony is excellent even though I probably would not like what they were singing. After the singing one of the officers, not the commander who is a baron, gave a typical German oration for a half hour. The enlisted men were drinking and singing all hours of the night that night. One of the favorite songs of the EM's is the "Beer Barrel Polka" which they sing in German. Another America song which they know is, "The Ferry Boat Serenade."

Next week our company is going to divide into two details. The detail for which I am listed is to go to Victoria, Kansas, which is ninety miles from here. There is supposed to be a college there were we will live while the hundered-twenty prisoners will live in a barn. We have be there for four to six weeks depending how long the harvesting may last. Another detail may go to Peabody which is two hundered miles away.

Friday another fellow and I were chasing prisoners on a farm 30 miles away at Glasco. The farm was very nice to us and gave us milk, mashed potatoes, hash, and cake, and coffee to add to lunch for us and the prisoners. The prisoners were shocking corn and did a good job of it.

I got the packages that you sent and thanks a lot. The sunglasses fit all right and were good on guard today. Thanks for the book too for we get enough time here to read so I ought to be able to finish it soon. Send more later if you have them.

You wanted to know how the food is. Well we have an excellent first cook who knows how to cook, especially pastry and rolls. Other wise we are getting good food but we are short on the meats that we enjoy the most.

I'm sorry to hear that Aunt Maude is so sick. Let me know how she is.

It is pouring now so I'm glad I didn't leave the barracks. We finally get paid this week, I hope. Write soon.

Love,
Donald

Postcards from Ft. Hays, Kansas

Saturday, Sept. 11, '43
Fort Hays Experiment Station, Hays, Kansas

Dear Mother and Dad,

We have really hit a rest camp now. A detail of fifty men and one hundered and twenty prisoners were sent out to side camp. I was a member of the twelve men who were sent out to be ready for the prisoners when they arrived. We left Concordia about nine thirty and got here about two thirty in the afternoon.

Andy Lieman and I rode on the truck carrying the mattresses so we could get some sleep if we wanted it. The scenery is very much the same mile after miles. Most of the ground is plowed for planted while the rest is still covered with corn shocks. Near Russell, Kansas, we passed and oil field. When we were in the middle of it all you could see were rows of wells that stretched to the horizon.

Hays is a fairly large town for this section of the country for we are only 67 miles from the Colorado border. It is a typically western town but there is the Kansas State College somewhere in town. We'll find out tonight as Lieman and I were on guard last night. Brant Taylor and another fellow that we pal around with, Bill Rockford, are on guard tonight. The prisoners arrived yesterday afternoon and after some indecision they were allowed to stay. Our lieutenant did not believe that the stockade would be finished, but the civilian who work at this experiment station did enough so the PW's could stay. The PW's are living in a barn and have another barn as a mess hall. We live in brick building that was formally a storage place for wheat seed and other grain.

This life is really easy as we are allowed to do guard duty in fatigues, except Sunday when the Colonel is expected, and to smoke on post to help keep us awake during the nights. The prisoners really like this place as well as we do as they use their limited vocabulary to say that is good. Before we were living on MP's rations which we limited in variety, but now we get our rations from Walker Air Field and that air corps really gets good food. The meal we had for lunch today was good enough for a Thanksgivings day dinner. We had ice tea and lemon, roast pork, (I ate five pork chops last night), corn on the cob, mashed potatoes and gravy, bread and jelly, and as many grapes as we could eat. I weigh about a hundered and sixty pounds now, but by the time we leave here which will probably be in four to six weeks I'll weigh a ton.

This experiment station is like a large farm as there are horses and four hundered head of cattle as well as farm land. The only thing we lack are showers which we should get this next week. Another detail was sent to Peabody, Kans., but they are probably leading a hard life. The cook is sick with gas poisoning, they are living in tents, and shaving out of their helmets. This is one detail where it paid to volunteer.

Last night we were paid and we were certainly glad to see it as everyone has been broke for some time. Everyone has been borrowing from everyone or anyone who had a dime in his pocket.

Write when you can and let me know how things are on the home front. Does Dad still have to work the long hours?

Love,
Donald

LAMER HOTEL, HAYS, KANS.

Sunday, September, 19, '43
Fort Hays Experiment Station, Hays, Kansas

Dear Mother and Dad,

I've completed another week in this army and again everything has settled to a routine of guard and prisoner chasing. During the day about hundered PW's are taken out by thirty of us MPEG's. The farmers are really treating the PW's and us very good. Several of the farmers are giving excellent meals at lunch, such as chicken and smoked ham. Today, Monday, another fellow and I had a home cooked meal as we were chasing prisoners on a farm. The PW's were really working hard today as they were shocking corn from 8:00 until 5:30 excluding an hour break at noon. The PW's enjoyed the same meal.
[Here in the letter there is an obvious change in the inks being used.]

The break in the letter was due to the fact that I was called out to guard the prisoners while they were exercising in one of the pastures. This week, we gave them a volleyball and they were playing a rough and tumble game similar to basketball only played in a field like soccer. Their favorite game is soccer but we don't have a soccer ball here. The Sunday before last the PW's were playing a game of baseball were they hit the runners with the ball to put the team out. These sports are interesting for us to watch.

Science Hall, F.H.K.S.C. Hays Kansas

Last night, Brant Taylor, Andy Lieman, Bill Rockford, and I went to town. Nothing to do but eat and go to a show. The air corps has practically ruined this town as far as liking soldiers goes. There is the Kansas State College here but most of the students are air corps trainees.

I got the package of newspapers and the Christmas Card during last week. Thanks for the newspapers as they are interesting to read during the days on guard. You had only better order 15 cards with my name on it but see if you can get more without the name at a cheaper price. If you can get another 15 for me and also 15 for Brant.

Incidentally, don't expect me home for sometime to come. After the first furloughs were issued all the rest were canceled by these side camps. Don't expect me home until I get there as that is the only way to take a furlough in the army. It is a case of take it when you get it and don't plan for it. Don't worry about me ever getting home for where there is will there is a way.

I received your last letter when I got in from chasing PW's today. Thanks for sending the cookies for that is always something that is well liked and can and will be eaten at any time. Most of the time cookies get here with two or three whole ones and the rest crumbs. Here is hoping that yours fair better. In regards to the books send them out whenever you have finished reading them. I've read "The Robe" but the other fellows will enjoy it. Send out any good books that you've got as I can generally find time to read them. A library is supposed to be starting in Concordia sooner or later so we ought to be able to get a book or two there. See if you get "Malta Story" as that sounds like an interesting book from what I read in the book section of the Tribune.

I'll have to close as the lights are going out in a minute or two. Write again soon.

Love,
Donald

P.S. When I get something to pack it in I'll return the Christmas card.

Sept. 29, 1943
Fort Hays Exp. Station, Hays, Kansas

Dear Mother and Dad,

Another month is just about over with and another pay day is only several days away. Tonight the Lt. gave us a talk asking us to buy some bonds for the third War Loan. I think I'll buy a twenty-five dollar one and have it sent home to you. I should get a full pay this month but I don't now how much it will be.

There is a good leather shop in town where they made all type of belts and etc. I ordered a garrison belt and a hand made wrist watch strap as a cheap one that I bought at Custer broke. I also bought several souvenir cowboy hats. I'll send them as soon as I am able to find a box to mail them in. Give one to Una as she like that type of thing.

The cookies arrived in good condition and were enjoyed by all. The newspapers got here yesterday and I was able to read them at that time as the prisoners were unable to work in the rain. It looked like rain today but it cleared off in the afternoon. Today Brant and I were given chicken for dinner. The farmer also gave us as much watermelon as we could eat. The melons they grow on that farm are really excellent and the PW's enjoy it as much as we do. We will really miss these meals when we return to Concordia. The work here will probably be finished in another two or three weeks as most of the large farms or ranch have most of the feed cut for season.

It is hard to write a letter around here to night as some of the fellows are playing with a volleyball in the barracks.
I'm glad to hear that Joey got a chance go into college training, tell me which college he is going to. Ernie said that he might be returning to Rutgers in several weeks. He'll be close to home which I can't expect as long as I am in the MPEG's.

I've had some pictures taken and I'll send them out as soon as I'm able. Be sure to sent those pictures that you took as soon as they are developed. I'll close for the present.

Love,
Donald

October 4, 1943
Fort Hays Exp. Station, Hays, Kansas

Dear Mother and Dad,

Here I am again, still in Kansas. I finally got a hold of some of the pictures that we have taken. We four have been palling around together since we got to Kansas. This picture was taken in front of the guard house at Concordia. The compounds are located to the left and in the back of the guard house although they can't be seen in the picture. All of the barracks are similar to the guard house and they don't look any too warm.

We have taken a number of pictures here in Hays and I should have some more that are better than these blown up photos. The fellow who took these did not know how to center the pictures very well. Yesterday we took pictures of the Germans and their stockade here in Hays. We also took several photos of the Kansas State College in town and I should get some copies in another week or two. Lieman took several pictures of us in OD's which should be pretty good.

Tonight I am on the third relief from one to five A.M. the worst hours of the night. I'll probably hit the hay early tonight to get some sleep. Today we went into town and spent a lot more of this months pay. Today I bought a garrison cap, stripes, and another tie. I suppose I'll have another job sewing the OD stripes of the winter woolens. I think I'll get a tailor to sew the stripes on my blouse and overcoat as they show the most. We are now allowed to wear the seventh corps area shoulder patch. The patch is a blue circle with a seven cornered star of white and another seven cornered star inside of that of blue. I've only put one on the blue as we can only get them by order and I've read that some of the corps areas were to be discontinued, although I have not heard about it in the army.

Besides buying the stuff I mentioned I got a hand made leather strap for my watch. The leather shop made up several of these as well as garrison belts. These belts and straps are made of good leather and probably cost less than the cheap stuff we would have gotten in other stores.

Tonight our detail presented the Lieutenant with a leather box to keep toilet articles in. We wanted to know if we were doing this so that we get furloughs. As yet we have not found out when we are to return to Concordia. The other side camp is to return October 23rd so it looks as if we may return even later. This winter there will probably be a number of side camps and the 480th will have first choice on them because of our experience.

Last night there was the first frost and from now on it is going to be cold out there on guard. One of the fellows wore an overcoat last night and I guess I'll get mine out soon.

Thanks a lot for the books and the candy which I got last week. The books will come in handy as I'll probably have to stay in quite a few nights this month. I also

Donald in Kansas

got your card today and suppose that your letter will get here tomorrow or the next day.

I'll be waiting for your next letter.

Love,
Donald

P.S. Lately all of the details have been shocking, just shocking. Four out five are shocking sorgum or cane for feeding the cattle this winter.

Thursday, Oct. 14, 1943
Ft. Hays Experiment Station, Hays, Kansas

Dear Mother and Dad,

He goes with another letter the first I have written since I wrote to you last week. I guess I'm getting very lazy in this type of outfit. I got your letter with all of the pictures in it some time ago. It was really swell to see how the people at home look at the present time. It looks like I'll have to buy some great big wallets like most of the Germans carry. Their wallets usually contain a group of pictures of themselves in the different campaigns and pictures of their families. One fellow showed me a group of pictures of Tunisian cities and some of the cities looked very beautiful.

Guard and prisoner chasing is still continuing as usual with nothing exciting ever happening. The PW's still like this detail and will be very sorry to see us return to Concordia. As yet, we don't know when we will return for every day the full limit of the prisoners are sent out to work. The PW's are still working on their usual policy of good eats & good work. Yesterday the farmer gave us a excellent meal of roast chicken, gravy, dressing, vegetables, & etc, so the PW's finished his twenty-seven acres and began working on another fellow's farm.

I am enclosing the war bond which I said that I bought. I think that I could spend twice as much money a month as they are willing to give me. I believe that I will have a certain amount taken out of my pay each month for bonds and then I know I'll be able to save some of the pay.

Have you taken up your job at the YW as yet. I imagine that you would let them talk you into a salary that they wanted to give you. I doubt if anything would even prevent you from taking the job. Are you still making preserves in the kitchen. I'll bet that they came out very good this year.

Well I pull guard again tonight. I think I'll close and write some other letters or try to get some sleep.

Love,
Donald

Saturday, October 16, 1943
Ft. Hays Experiment Station, Hays, Kansas

Dear Mother and Dad,

Well, here I am on guard again tonight so I thought I'd write before I put it off for another week. Fall weather has arrived in Kansas as the nights are very cold (freezing lately) and all of the trees are beginning to turn red and yellow. I finally got around to mailing those souvenir hat today when I went into town for a hair cut. You will probably get the package some time next week.

One of the fellows who is here in Hays is getting an emergency furlough. He lives in New Brunswick and he said that he would probably be going to Dunellen while he is home. Incidentally, his name is P.f.c. Carl Rovenish. I'll give him this letter and he'll mail it when he gets to New York on Monday so that you will get it on Tuesday. Carl said that he would probably stop in at our house early Tuesday if it were possible. He'll probably be able to give you a good idea of what we are going out here in Kansas.

Next week end we are returning to Concordia. I'm sure we will be sorry to leave this easy detail here at Hays. We are all hoping that we will be sent out on another detail as soon as possible. The rumor factory is now beginning to think up new places for us to go. Some officers are going out to inspect this side camp. They are from the seventh service command and this may have bearing on our next assignment.

So Lew Kirchner is in the army now. Oh, well, it could happen to anybody. Incidentally I bought a good leather strap for my watch here at Hays. It is a handmade strap and goods pretty good so I won't need a metal wrist band for a while. I could use one or two of those sleeveless sweaters as it gets plenty cold out here in Kansas. I could also use a good pair of leather dress gloves sometime or other.

You said that Joey is home on a furlough but where is he stationed now. Send me Una's and Frank's address as I might catch up on my letter writing some day.

Here are some pictures and I'll send some more when I get more money and reprints. Even the PW's want some pictures of the four of us.

I'll close now and give the letter to Carl.

Love,
Donald

P.S. Also best wishes on your anniversary twenty-one years and still going strong.

Back of photo:
Roxie, Andy, Don
and Brant

Sunday, October 24, 1943
Ft. Hays Experimental Station, Hays, Kansas

Dear Mother and Dad,

Another Sunday has rolled around and we are still in Hays. Friday night we were informed by the Lieutenant that we were going back to Concordia on Monday and that we were to pack Sunday. When I brought in the PW's Saturday we were told that we would be here for Monday at least. We still don't know whether we will return to Concordia on Tuesday or when. The other detail which is at Peabody has not returned and expects to stay there all winter. What will happen to our detail depends on the colnel and the War Department. We have been working as usual and by now we have shocked most of the feed for this county and the next. More work is being done in town though and most of the PW's are working every day. Saturday I had some stone masons who were putting a foundation under a house.

I got the last letter this morning, and the package of newspapers and German books arrived during the week. Those books will come in handy this winter when I don't have anything else to do. That dollar you sent will come in handy this month. The four of us have been about broke as we bought bonds and a lot of clothes. You don't have to worry about me gambling as you can't do it when you're broke or you find that you can't win anyway. Pay day is at the end of this week so I don't have to stretch that dollar much farther. Incidentally, a special delivery letter doesn't get here any faster than airmail, while air mail beats regular mail by a day or a day and a half.

I'm glad to see that you were able to sell the car as it was doing no one any good any way. I got the letter from Alfred Day today and I'll have the thing returned in several days. I won't need the extra money at the beginning of the month so keep it until half the month has gone by. I'll buy some more clothes if we stay in Hays, but probably not as many as last month.

It is too bad that you missed seeing Carl Rovenish as he is quite talkative and can speak German excellently. For this reason he probably knows the PW's better than most of us. This morning, we had our picture taken by the fellow who is superintendent at this experimental farm. It is a group picture of our detail and I hope that I'll be able to get a copy of it. I'll send some more pictures after payday as we took some a couple of weeks ago. It is as hard to get film here as it is in the East but Concordia generally has a supply of film. I'll enclose some picture postcards of Hays so that you'll get an idea of the town.

As I should write a bunch of letters before I go on guard tonight I'll close this letter. I hope I don't freeze tonight as the nights are cold while the days are still quite warm.

With love to all,
Donald

Detail of Donald squatting in front on the left

Group picture of guard detail at Ft. Hays Experiment Station Larger picture on next page

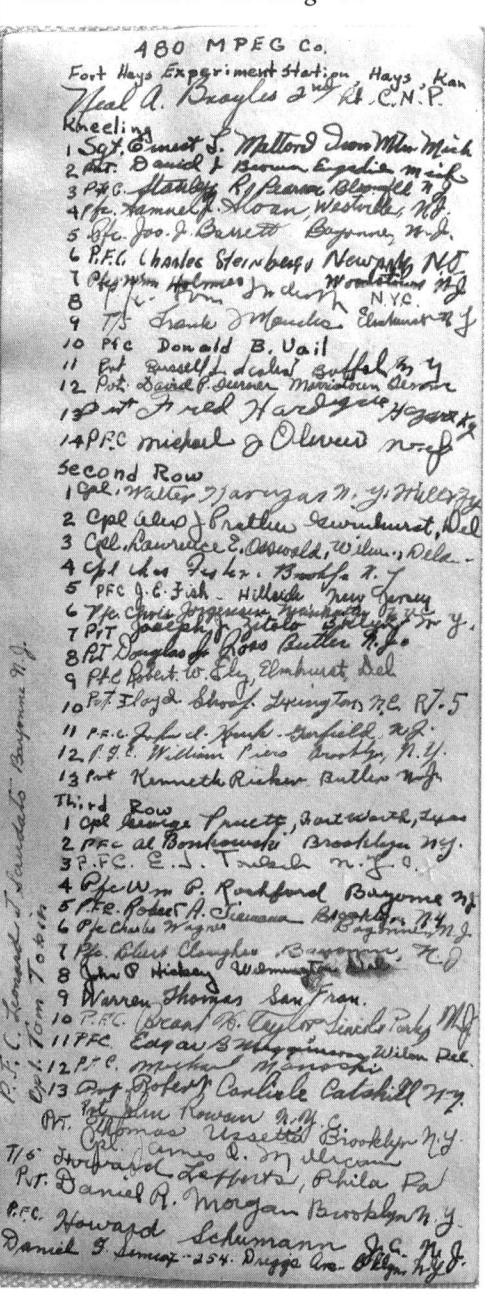

Guard detail at Ft. Hays Station

Back of photo with guards' names written presumably in their own hand. Donald is "Kneeling #10"

480 MPEG Co.
Fort Hays Experiment Station, Hays, Kan.
Neal A. Baayles 2nd Lt. C.M.P.

Kneeling
1 Sgt. Ernest J. Mellord Dearn Mtn. Mich.
2 Pvt. Donald J. Brown Empelie mich
3 PFC. Stanley R. Pearar Blondel N.J
4 Pfc. Samuel J. Sloan Westville, N.J.
5 Pfc. Jos. J. Barrett Bayonne, N.J.
6 P.F.C. Charles Steinberg Newark, N.J
7 Pfc. Wm Holmes Jackson Woodstown N.J
8 Pvt. McClosky N.Y.C.
9 T/5 Frank J Meneles Elizabeth N.J
10 Pfc Donald B. Vail
11 Pvt Russell J Sicdal Buffalo N.Y
12 Pvt. David P. Turner Morristown Jerone
13 Pvt Fred Hardy Hozant Ky
14 PFC Michael J Oliveri N.J.C.

Second Row
1 Cpl. Walter J Harrigas N.Y. Willy
2 Cpl Alex J Prather Swindhurst, Del.
3 Cpl. Lawrence E. Oswald, Wilm., Dela.
4 Cpl Ches Fester Brooklyn N.J.
5 PFC J.C. Fish - Hillside New Jersey
6 T/5 Chris Joggreen Woodstown N. Y.
7 Pvt Joseph J Pitelo Brooklyn N.Y
8 Pvt Douglas J Ross Butler N. J.
9 Pfc Robert W. Ely Elmhurst Del.
10 Pvt Floyd Shoaf Lexington N.C. R.7.5
11 P.F.C. John A. Hauk Garfield N.J.
12 P.9.C. William Piero Brooklyn N.Y.
13 Pvt Kenneth Ricker Butler N.J.

Third Row
1 Cpl George Pruitt, Fort Worth, Texas
2 PFC al Bonkowski Brooklyn N.Y.
3 P.F.C. E.J. Toleth N.J.C.
4 Pfc Wm P. Rochford Bayonne N.J
5 Pfc. Robert A. Sienma Brooklyn N.Y
6 Pfc Charles Wagner Bayonne N.J
7 Pfc Elert Clougher Bayonne N.J
8 John P. Hickey Wilmington Del.
9 Warren Thomas San Fran.
10 P.F.C. Brant B. Taylor Lincoln Park N.J
11 Pfc Edgar B Higgins Wilm. Del.
12 Pfc Michael Manoski
13 Pvt Robert Carlisle Catskill N.Y
Pvt John Rowan N.Y.
Cpl Thomas Ussette Brooklyn N.Y.
T/5 Howard James J. McIlvain
Pvt Daniel Lefferts, Phila Pa.
P.F.C. Howard R. Morgan Brooklyn N.Y.
Daniel J. Semos - 254 Dugge Ave. Bklyn N.J.

P.F.C. Armand J Sautsato Bayonne N.J.
Cpl Tom Tobin
63

Monday, November 8, 1943
Prisoner of War Camp, Concordia, Kansas

Dear Mother and Dad,

Well, here I am again. No, your wandering boy did not get lost. We returned to Concordia from Hays last Monday in fairly high spirits. The gang expected pay and perhaps furloughs, but all we got was pay. Several fellows got furloughs and the captain said the rest of us would get them as soon as possible. The balance of last week was spent chasing prisoners as we did not have enough men at the time. I'll enclose one of the worksheets that the prisoners give to us for the day.

Some of the things have changed since we were away. Now the prisoners are allowed to roam around the camp with the outside of the area guarded. The prisoners are doing K.P. and are latrine orderlies so they are doing the hardest work around here. The hardest job is trying to keep warm for it is beginning to get cold in Kansas. Yesterday it was snowing and the wind was blowing and that cold was really cutting. Today was just as cold and we put on all the clothes we had when we went out for a few minutes of drill. For the balance of the day we had classes on guns and an hour or so on German. We are learning the more common phrases and words and if we can get some practice we ought to understand it.

Tomorrow night we begin to pull guard again as more men returned from Peabody although the prisoners and some of the fellows are still there. The fourth guard company was sent here from Custer, so we will pull guard every four days and the same for prisoner chasing. We have been issued a lot of winter clothing and I hope it will keep us warm up in the towers. We also were given gloves, a scarf, sweater, and knit helmet by the Red Cross besides our regular G.I. clothes.

I finally got the last package that you sent. Thanks for the papers and cards. What is the score on those cards now? How much do they cost as I don't remember the prices? Am I supposed to get some more cards with my name on them or not. Brant sends his thanks and will pay me as soon as I find out the price.

So now your making more money at the "Y". Now I imagine that your finding trouble trying to find places to spend it, Mother. Perhaps you spend all of your time making it, rather than spending it.

I'll close now and I'll make the letters closer together now that we are back in Concordia and settling into the usual routine.

Love,
Donald

P.S. Thanks for selling the car.

Mother

Monday, November 15, 1943
Prisoner of War Camp, Concordia, Kan.

Dear Mother and Dad,

I'm on prisoner chasing today and I have been lucky for the second straight prisoner chasing day. The last time I had a detail that was working in the stockade so I did not have to work except for an hour in the afternoon when I and another fellow got a town detail of 8 PW's to unload a freight car. The same will probably happen today, I hope so. Saturday night we pulled guard so I was in tower #13 on the 13th. They brought in eight war dogs Saturday night and they were kept across the road. At least they help keep you awake and you really need something with two on and four off.

Our original company is beginning to break up more and more. We lost the first ones in Custer and quite a few been transferred here in Concordia. Saturday three fellows received orders to report to Greenville, Pa on Dec. 1. They leave tonight on a delayed journey which is better than a furlough as your tickets are bought and meal paid for. One of the fellows was Bill Rockford so the first of the four of us was able to get out of the MPEG's. He didn't expect the transfer, but he and the other fellows were mail clerks before they entered the army. Now they will go to school for four months and then get a new assignment. I guess I still have a chance to get some engineering, maybe. Brant is still hoping to be transferred to the air corps. The replacements are fellows who have been kicked out of other outfits, physically unfit for other duty, or have been replaced by the Wac's.

I got letters from Una and Aunt Elvretta. It was nice to hear about Plainfield. Aunt Elvretta told me about her family, while Una told me of her honeymoon. I just received a box of nut fudge from Aunt Bess and it sure is excellent and the boys are enjoying it. Uncle Roy sent me two boxes of salt water taffy last week from Atlantic City.

Well, I have spent two hours on area guard and eaten lunch since the last paragraph. Perhaps I'll get the afternoon off, I hope. The area guard is only during the day while the prisoners are working in the camp area. The PW's also go to see some of the American movies and yesterday it looked silly to see one guard behind three hundered Germans.

I suppose that both of us are still working hard but it is good thing you like the work. Write when you get the chance.

Love,
Donald

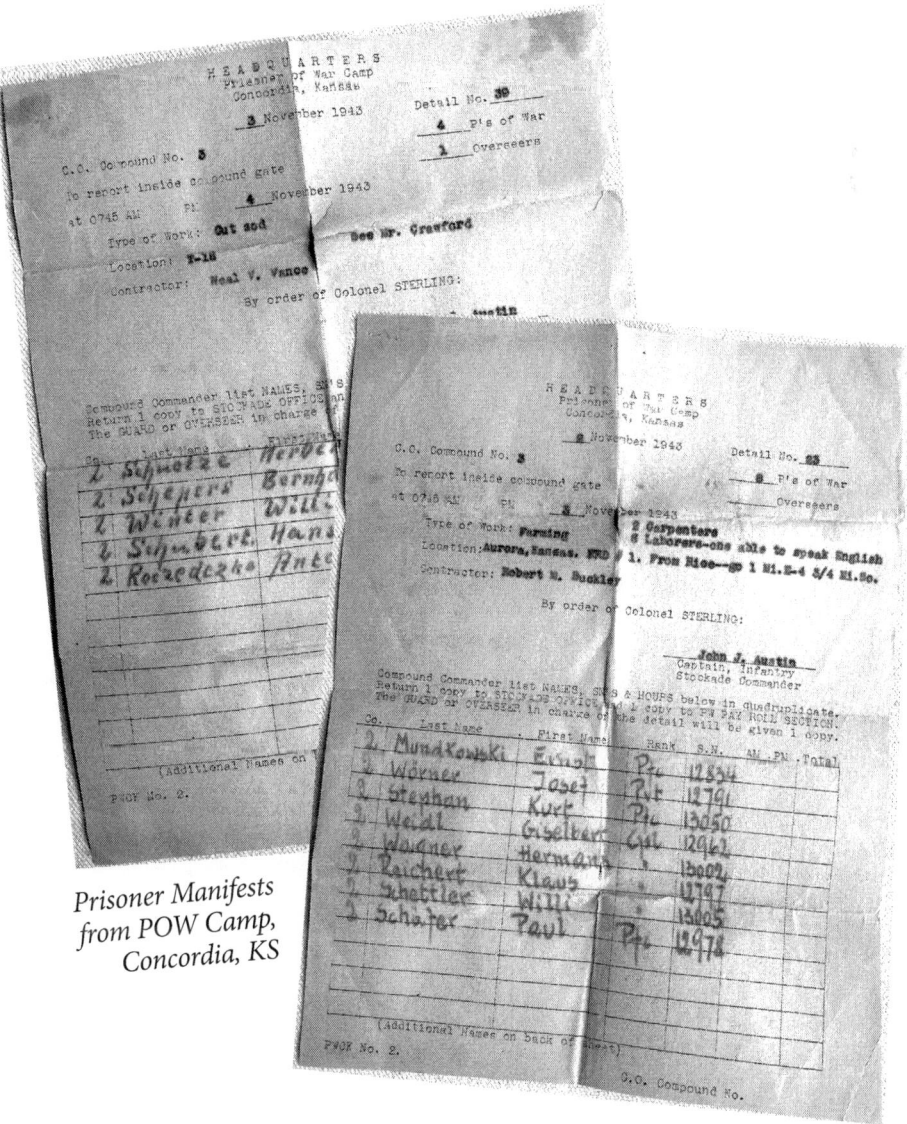

Prisoner Manifests from POW Camp, Concordia, KS

Sunday, November 21, 1943
Prisoner of War Camp, Concordia, Kansas

Dear Mother and Dad,

I received your letter and package in yesterday's mail. Thanks a lot for the sweater, cards, and newspapers. Don't worry about the size of the sweater as it is generally worn over a lot of clothes. Actually I don't need it now as we were issued a lot of winter woolen but it will come in handy as a dress sweater worn under the blouse. I see that your still the same business women as usual as you sold the radio to pay for the Xmas cards. You had better watch the way that wrap the packages, Mother. Several of them have been ripped open although nothing has been lost.

Thanks for the five dollars from the sale of the car. It will probably come in handy before the end of this month. It is a shame that you missed Roxie as he probably told you a lot about what we are doing. He got his lucky break and I ought to get mine before long.

I received the box of fudge and cookies from Aunt Bess. Thank her for me if you see her soon.

We are on guard this afternoon and I have the second relief on the two on and four off schedule. We are luck if we get five hours sleep with this arrangement. We also are due to pull guard on Thanksgiving night. The way it works out we are due to be off at five o'clock on December 24th so we will be off for Christmas. This would then put us on New Years Eve although this is still a long ways off.

I see that you are still busy at the "Y". I suppose that you like it as much as ever.

I'll close now as we have to clean up before we go on guard. It is fairly warm this afternoon although we will probably freeze to death tomorrow morning in those towers.

Love,
Donald

December 10, 1943
Prisoner of War Camp, Concordia, Kansas

Dear Mother and Dad,

My address will soon be changed from Kansas, I hope. The sergeant told me today that my application for ASTP had been accepted at the seventh service command headquarters at Omaha. He said that this was quick work and that I would probably be transferred within a weeks time. As this is the case, mother, you had better not send any packages to this address other than those that you may have mailed. If you send any more packages they will only be kicking around in the mails until I am finally established in some college.

I have found out that applicants are sent to a star unit in Grinnell, Iowa. I guess this is the correct spelling of the town's name. You receive the aptitude test here to see if you are qualified and are then sent to some college. With my

Christmas card signed "from the officers and men of the 480th"

qualifications I ought to be able to get into advanced engineering and this would give me nine months of college. This would be all right with me. Brant as finally decided that he would try for ASTP as he has been told that it would be practically impossible to get in the air corps. He will get it if he is able to get past the company commander.

I arrived here early Thursday morning and got about two hours sleep. Last night I was put on guard with another company and tomorrow night I'll pull it with our company. All of the companies except one have details of men out so everyone pulls guard about every other day. The train trip was unadventful except for talking to a few people and meeting a couple of our fellows in Chicago. I had a double seat from Chicago to New York so I got some sleep there. There wasn't any need to have worried about the reservations in New York as I was able to get one in Chicago.

I'll send out the Christmas cards on Sunday night and will write you another letter before I leave here. Write as soon as possible or the letter will be kicked around.

Love,
Donald

P. S. I got paid today so there is no need to worry about money.

ASTP

Army Specialized Training Program

Grinnell College, Grinnell, Iowa
and the University of Tennessee,
Knoxville, Tennessee

Saturday, December 18
Grinnell College, Grinnell, Iowa

Dear Mother and Dad,

I am finally back to college again. Two other fellows and myself left Concordia last night and arrived here at Grinnell. One fellow is a company clerk from one of the other guard companies while the other fellow was originally in our company. This fellow and I bunked together the short time that we were in the 474 MPEG Co at Custer but was later transferred from the 480 to act as librarian at Concordia. He is trying for languages here.

As things appear to be from what we have found out we will probably begin to take tests Monday. First we will be given an orientation lecture and then different tests on the subject that we desire. I won't have any difficulty in getting into basic engineering but I would like to get into advanced so that I won't lose my stripe. All basic men lose their stripes while advanced men keep all they have or are given a PFC. After you are finished you are given a "T" under the stripe making you a T6 (Technician 6th Grade) (no more pay) and are sent to another outfit, where if ratings are available, you are promoted to higher technicians grades.

I went into town tonight but it is a small college town and there was very little to due. The town is very much like Concordia. We went to the USO and addressed Christmas cards and came back to the dormitories. Everyone must be in at ten o'clock every night for bed check but no one complains in this town. Perhaps I'll be able to get a pass next weekend and go to Chicago or Des Moines. Chicago is five hours away and Des Moines only two.

After the test an interview is given and this may wash out border line cases. After you are accepted a refresher course is given until it is time for another shipment. Shipments are sent out when enough fellows are ready. Enclosed are some pictures of the college.

Enclosed is also a money order for thirty dollars to help pay for the twin beds. Perhaps it will help to pay back some of the money I used while I was home of the furlough. Mother, there is a package in the mails for you but you probably won't receive it until after Christmas. Write to the address on the envelope but don't send any packages if I'll have to carry to gift.

Love and Merry Christmas
Donald

Postcard of the men's dormitory at Grinnell College

Monday, December 27
Grinnell College, Grinnell, Iowa

Dear Mother and Dad,

Another Christmas has come and gone for which I imagine that you are very thankful because of the usual disorder of things. I hope that it turned out to be a merry one even though I could not be there. Some of the fellows went home to New York on three day passes but I don't know how much they were able to enjoy it as the train schedule would only leave them a very few hours at home. Many of the fellows went to Chicago and to Des Moines over the week end but I and one of my roommates decided to stay here at the College.

As it was we had an enjoyable time and excellent meals as there were a few soldiers in town. Over the week end we had steak twice and Christmas dinner with turkey and all of the trimmings. There was a dance in the USO in the afternoon and the balance of the time we went to see movies in town. I worked a few hours Friday and Sunday mornings as mail clerk so I was able to get my mail and packages as soon as they arrived at headquarters. Your package arrived via Concordia on Sunday morning so Sunday seemed more like Christmas to me.

Thanks so very much for everything that you sent me. All of the presents were really swell and fun guessing what was in them before you open the package. Among the fellows in our room we have enough candy and cookies and such to last us for the rest of the winter. One of the fellows who went to Baltimore on his pass has about nine pounds of candy and nuts besides three or four boxes of cake and cookies.

Today I received the package of goodies from aunt Ruth and Uncle Lou. This only adds to our supply so we are really stocked up. I also opened on Christmas a package from Aunt Bess and Uncle Pete containing a tie and handkerchief. Aunt Clara and Uncle Elmer sent me some money so all in all, it was a Merry Christmas here in Iowa. Thank them all and I will try to write to thank them personally soon as possible.

Up until now I have been living the life of Riley here in college. We get up at quarter of six, reveillery at six, and then make the beds with two sheets and clean the room for inspection before seven o'clock when we eat breakfast. The fellows going to refresher courses fall out at 7:25 but we stay here until eight o'clock, when we we take calisthenics for an hour followed by a shower. Later on have an hour of close order drill and possibly a half hour class or lecture on some subject. We eat lunch at 11:30 and fall out again at one for mass athletics, generally football, but today we went over the obscale course twice. The day is generally finished unless there is another half hour class. We stand retreat at 5:30 and eat supper afterwards. Light are supposed to be out at 10:30 although everyone is to be in the room at ten o'clock.

We have been leading that type of easy life (except on some on used muscles) because we have not been processed. Tomorrow we are to be given an orientation lecture to find out what you desire and that will be followed by the general tests. Afterwords we will be interviewed to tell us if we have passed. Then refresher courses are given until the day that you are shipped out. That shipping day might be any day after you are accepted when a college orders a certain number of a certain classification of student. In our room there are two fellows in basic engineering, one who graduated from Cornell in mechanical engineering here about two months, and another here six weeks awaiting assignment to a pre-dental college.

Chances are that I'll be shipped before the fifteenth of January when most semesters begin. There are only a few advanced engineers here then again it may be indefinite. At least you know where you are going for you make out the tags for your barracks bags before you leave.

I'll close now and hope that I'll receive a letter telling me of Christmas at home.

Happy New Year with all my love,
Donald

January 3, 1944
Grinnell College, Grinnell, Iowa

Dear Mother and Dad,

Here is my first letter of the New Year and it contains some good news. I have finally been accepted for ASTP. Last Tuesday we were given our first test on psychology and asked for college or high school records. Those trying for advanced work were then given the advanced tests on Thursday. These tests include the tests on the different branches of math, physics, and chemistry and lasted for a day and a half averaging three hours each.

Today we were given our final interview by a civilian psychology professor at Grinnell and an army leiutenant. Quite a few of the fellows passed while another few flunked out and will be sent back to their own companies. I was fairly sure that I was in, as the board began asking me about the work I had been doing and were interested in the attitude of the Germans and how our camp was operated. Finally they came back to the subject by asking me where I fit in the program. I said that I would like mechanical engineering, and the fourth term although I had messed up the calculus test a little. They said that was true although I would have a chance to get a week to four weeks refresher on differential calculus here in Grinnell and would have to take integral calculus which is a part of the fourth term. The board said that my test marks were above average and that I would be accepted for term four.

I'll now have to wait around here until shipping order come thru for the advanced students. I may be shipped out soon as there are quite a few fellows in advanced who have been here for five or six weeks. If I am not shipped out this or next week I'll be here for another month. There will be fellows shipped east within the next couple of weeks as many colleges have terms beginning this month and I sure would like it if I ever hit any of those groups.

When you go down to Mikus's store thank Mr. and Mrs. Mikus for me. They sent me a fruit cake and it really was excellent when we eat it. It was sent out to Hays, then Concordia, but I finally got it and it was still in excellent condition. Aunt Gladys and Uncle Russ sent me a package which I received last week. They sent me cigarettes, a leather cigarette case, and candy. There is also some else you can thank for me if you see them. Aunt Clara sent me a subscription to Readers Digest.

As long as I may be here a while find my slide rule, put a little tissue paper around the slide rule and fill up the space so that the slide index glass will not slide and break. See if you can find the green box in the attic that it came in and pack it in there. Wrap the box with corrigated paper and then wrap with paper and make sure that it is tied good and tight. Insure it for fifteen dollars and mail it here. Thanks again.

It has been beautiful around here for two days last week and again today. It started with a foggy day and very cold. The fog seems to settle on the trees and bushes and freeze. The trees are then coated with a beautiful white frost so that they seem to be as pretty as a picture. It reminds me of the bushes that you paint white and sprinkle with snow.

We had to work all day New Years Day as we usually do around here. Inspection, exercise, drill, and sports. In the afternoon we had our own football game between the fellows in our company. I was on the team that won by the score of 30 to 24. We had to be in at 10:00 on New Years Eve although we played cards until late.

I close now as I have to dress for the obstacle course this afternoon.

With all my love,
Donald

Sunday, January 9, 1944
Grinnell College, Grinnell, Iowa

Dear Mother and Dad,

Another week has passed and the possibilities have been increased that I will stay here for another month. Most of the colleges were beginning on the tenth of January so a few of the fellows were shipped out. None of the basics were shipped and those who have finished refreshers will now get a short furlough but the advanced are eligible for shipment on any day. The fellows who were 9A or have degrees were shipped to the University of Minnesota where they will take a three months course. Fellows in odd number terms were shipped out this week. It is too bad that I was not shipped here several weeks earlier as I would have been shipped with the other "fours" who went to M.I.T. What a college that would have been to be assigned to.

This program seems to be slowing done quite a bit as they are tightening the requirements even more than they were. In the last group processed only about 40% were accepted while the rest are to be returned to their companies. There is a large number of fellows pilling up here awaiting shipment to colleges so that is one of the reasons for giving furloughs.

I received your long letter during the week and it was swell to hear of Christmas at home. Incidentally I received the money for my birthday just before I left Concordia and I thought that I had thanked you for it. We were given a partial payment this week of twenty dollars. I imagine that this town really had trouble trying to cash all of those twenty dollar bills in one night.
The box from the church also arrived before I left Concordia. I'll try to write Mr. Palmer early this week to thank him.

I received a letter from Rite today telling me of her trip to visit Lew. Mr. & Mrs. Sullivan's card contained a short note asking to stop there again if I ever had the chance.

I'll close now hoping you'll write soon as you're not as busy as you were before and during Christmas.

As ever, Love,
Donald

Monday, January 17, 1944
Grinnell College, Grinnell, Iowa

Dear Mother and Dad,

I received the slide rule last week and it came thru in perfect shape. Thanks very much for sending it so soon after I asked for it. It really comes in handy when ever there is some math problem to work. I am still taking the calculus and physics and sleeping during the two study hours.

I took a week end pass this week and went into Des Moines. The pass was good from six PM Saturday until ten PM Sunday evening. The Rock Island R. R. runs from here to Des Moines so I was on the same Rocket that I would have taken to go to Concordia. We had to stand but I was glad that I was not returning to Concordia. There were four of us that went together and one of these fellows was from Plainfield. His name is Van Nemen and lived on Madison Ave and went to Rutgers for a while.

We took double rooms in fairly good hotel and went out and had fun. At one time during the evening we met some Wac's and about half of them were from New Jersey. They lived in Jersey City, Asbury Park, New Brunswick, and Netherwood while the others were from the Middle West. We slept until late Sunday, ate, and went to the U.S.O. for a while. Later on I went skating and to a show. I spent quite a bit of money but we were given a partial payment here and I still had money left from Concordia and Christmas. I may go there again next week end if I am still here.

A large number of fellows were shipped in today but as yet Brant has not been sent here. I wrote to him last week but if the company has gone to Minnesota I don't know when I'll get answer or when he'll get here.

I received a letter from Joe Houska today telling me that he had failed to be accepted as an air cadet for navigator. I guess he really would have liked it. Bud says that if things go okeh he should get his wings late in February.

Here is a clipping about the old camp. I think that most of the cases are new. Write when you can.

Love,
Donald

Monday, January 24, 1944
Grinnell College, Grinnell Iowa

Dear Mother and Dad,

As you can see I am still here in Grinnell. There have not been any shipments and in fact there are not any rumors of any. Everything goes on as usual as no new men have been shipped here for classification.

I got the newspapers early last week and enjoyed reading them. You might as well send "Bedside Esquire" out here as there is plenty of time to read which I probably won't have when I leave here. Send out the college physics (Hausman & Slack) book too, so that I may look it over. I'll send for some of the other books when ever I am sent to a college.

Last Wenesday I was C.Q. (Charge of Quarters) so now I have two of the three details that you can get here. K. P. is the only one I have not had but I can only get it on a weekend (Sunday) as I have classes all the rest of the time.

I received a letter from bud last week and he said that he had only four more weeks of training to go. His new nickname is the "Flame" because he had the least errors in bombing, in his class. His only worry is that they will keep him there as an instructor.

Brant also wrote last week and told me that the 480th was getting prepared for overseas shipment. They received rush orders on the 9th to be in New York on the 12th but fifteen men were still on furloughs including Brant and Andy. The company asked for an extension so an East Coast company was sent. The 480th is really taking a beating. They are pulling guard, drilling, ten & more mile hikes, and everything else Fort Custer style. As yet I am on detached service so they are not shipping for a while. One of the fellows in my room was attached to the AST unit here so that his company could come up to full strength. He was also in the MPEG's.

I'll probably go to Des Moines again next week unless something turns up. Write when you can.

Love,
Donald

Thursday, Feb 3, 1944
Univ. of Tennessee, Knoxville, Tennessee

Dear Mother and Dad,

As you can see from my new address I have finally been shipped from Grinnell. Everything was going on as usual until last Friday when the inside rumors began to spread. I decided that I might as well go to Des Moines for it would probably be the last time before I shipped. I went with the two other fellows who came with me from Concordia and we had a good time skating and roaming around.

On Monday morning after breakfast the shipping list was read. I and another fellow were to go to the University of Tennessee, one to Purdue, some to V.M.I., and 39 basics to Baylor Univ. Waco, Tex. Included in this group was Suess, the fellow in our room who lived in Baltimore. A couple of hours later 39 more basics were called to be shipped to C.C.N.Y. in New York City and so three more fellows from our room went to New York. One of the fellows lives in the Western part of Virginia and has his girl here in Knoxville so I said I would call her if he would call you and tell you were I was going. His name is I. F. Burke and is a very nice fellow.

All of the fellows headed East left afternoon so we had a private car while some Naval aviation cadets had another. I turned in my passport to the Midwest when we crossed to Mississippi at Rock Island. In Chicago the different groups broke up heading for their own college.

We had to spend all of our time in Chicago making reservations for a pullman to Cinniatti. Perhaps I'll get to see some part of that town besides the railroad stations. Mike Hardin, the fellow I was traveling with, lived near Cinniatti so we stopped there for a few hours before we left for Knoxville. We arrived in Knoxville at three o'clock in the morning and had a little trouble finding out where we were to go as the AST Unit is rather small while the air corps has a large detachment here awaiting classification.

I'm now down in the South for a while and I'll probably be speaking with a drawl the next time you see me. There is nothing to do this week except take a pass and go into town or stay in the barracks and write or sleep.

I received your letter on Monday telling about Bud's mother. It is to bad that it had to happen to her for Dunellen will not seem the same whenever Bud or I are home. I'll write to Bud some time today for I believe that he will be back in Childress by now.

Here is hoping that for the next nine months my address will remain the same. Write when you can.

Love,
Donald

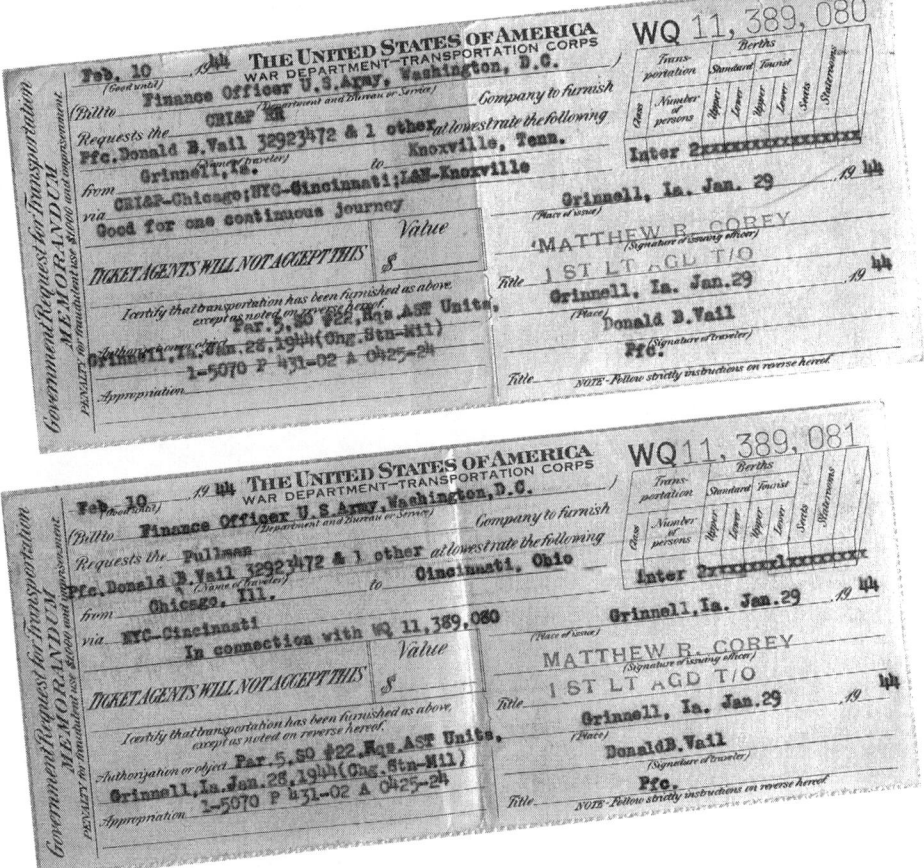

Army train passes

Saturday, Feb. 12, 1944
Univ. of Tennessee, Knoxville, Tennessee

Dear Mother and Dad,

We began classes last Monday and now the first week has been completed except for a personal inspection by the Major in a half hour. We will be able to get our passes and go into town after that and it will be nice to have some free time after a week of constant study. We are not allowed to go any where during the week except to the restaurant to eat and to the library at night to study.

It is a good thing that I have been to college before because they are throwing the subjects at us very fast although they are covering all of the work. The only subjects that I have not had before our thermodynamics and military science, but neither have been hard as yet. The profs give us a lot of work and tell us to do as much as possible. We get a number of small quizzes and I have good marks in those I've taken so far. The other subjects on the list are shop, drawing, mechanics, and calculus.

I received a letter from uncle Roy on Monday with my new address on it. That was quick service. He said that he would be in Johnson City until the 25th when he will return to New Jersey. I'll probably go up to visit him next week if I have the money. This means I'd like to borrow about five or six dollars until next pay day. I'll be paid all of the money that is owing me then so I'll have some spending money.

I won't need any of the books for a while, but if you have not shipped for physics book you might include the mechanics book and the Mechanical Engineering Handbook. If you would they would be handy to check up on the other books that we have here.

I have not heard from Bud since he returned to Texas but I imagine that he is busy catching up so that he will graduate this month. I have not heard from Brant lately either.

Write when you can. I hope the "YW" is not keeping you too busy, Mother, and the shop, Dad.

As always,
Love,
Donald

Friday, February 18, 1944
Univ. of Tennessee, Knoxville, Tenn.

Dear Mother and Dad,

I have just enough time to write to you before lights are out. I received the registered letter yesterday. Thanks a lot for the money that you have sent me for it will probably last me to pay day as my laundry did not cost as much as I expected. I'll get off tomorrow about three o'clock and I should get into Johnson City a little before eight o'clock and met Uncle Roy there. I hope that everything will turn out all right.

The physics books arrived from Grinnell this week. The other books will probably arrive this week if you have mailed them. I hope I don't have to return them before long. We just heard the report over the radio that the ASTP would be cut by 110 000 by April first. Everyone around here is considering getting out their manuals on the Garand rifle, infantry, and other branches of the service.

This week I have been a cadet second lieutenant. There is very little work to do during the week, but on Saturday there is a company inspection and drill. I hope it rains or snows it has every other day this week. Perhaps if I can get enough experience in drilling I'll get to be a corporal some day. I've had some experience in marching our section to restaurant this week.

In answering one of your questions we live in barracks, but these are better constructed and better heated than the ones we had in Kansas. The 1,200 air corps students here live in the dormitories, gym, and grand-stands.

It is too bad about Mrs. Frazee but don't get into any trouble worrying about her, Mother.

I'll close now so I can listen to the news on the radio as it is ten o'clock. Write when you have the chance.

Love,
Donald

Thursday, March 2, 1944
Univ. of Tenn., Knoxville, Tenn

Dear Mother and Dad,

I don't think that I have written you since I said that was going to visit uncle Roy. As it happened I did not see him although I started out for Johnson City. After I got my pass I was able to get down town in time to get the ticket and wait for the bus. I waited quite a while after the bus was supposed to have left and then found out that no bus was going to leave for some reason unknown at the time in the bus station. The next bus into Johnson City would have gotten to me there quite late so I decided to telegram Uncle Roy and tell him that I could not make it. He wrote me from Plainfield that he was sorry that he did not see me.

The time is really flying fast with all of the work that we have to do. Before we know it another weekend has rolled around. This week the engineering students are giving a banquet downtown. I think I'll go with the fellow I have been going around with. His name is Bud MacFarland and comes from Oak Park which is next to Chicago. He is studying electrical engineering.

I received a card from Bud Thatcher this week. It was an announcement of the graduation of his class and enclosed was also a personal calling card with the name Charles B. Thatcher 2nd Lieutenant USAAF. I'll probably hear from him later this week or next telling whether he is to due instruction or further training Ed Pyatt wrote and told me that all of the fellows except twenty where being sent back to the troops. He has been at Washington Univ. in St. Louis in basic but now I suppose he'll have to go back to the medics.

We were paid this week and I'll send a money order as some as I can get one. I'll have to find out if I can get one thru the postal clerk or if I'll have to go down town.

I'll close now as I have to do a little studying for a military science test this afternoon.

Love,
Donald

Wenesday, March 8, 1944
Univ. of Tenn., Knoxville, Tenn.

Dear Mother and Dad,

Another week has past and time is really rolling on. We seldom have much time to think about it as there is so much work to due. I am really behind in my letter writing as I have a stack of them in front of me that have to be answered.

The papers arrived on Monday so I spent most of my spare time on that day reading them. Thanks for sending them to all of the time as it is interesting to know what is doing around the area.

I finally got around to getting the money order today. It is made out to dad so you will have to get it cashed. Take ten or fifteen dollars out for you, Mother, as I imagine that the last money that you sent me came from you. The balance may be considered a payment on the money I borrowed on my last furlough or credited for the next one, when ever that may be. This term is supposed to end somewhere near the end of April and we should get a week off as long as the program keeps going.

I went to the engineer's banquet last Friday given by the civilian students in downtown Knoxville. It was very interesting although we could not appreciate all of the humor as we did not know all of the professors although we did know many of them. The mechanicals won the contest between the engineering societies on the humorous sketches. They had a quintets singing parodies about engineering subjects and the professors. The weather changed last night and we had snow flurries although most of the time it has been warm. I have seen more rain here than any other place since I have been in the army.

I'll close now to write a few more letters.

Love,
Donald

Sunday, March 19, 1944
University of Tennessee, Knoxville, Tenn.

Dear Mother and Dad,

It is another rainy weekend in Knoxville for the past six Saturdays it has rained on five and now the rain is continuing all day Sunday. Generally we have to carry our raincoats on weekends as we know it will be raining by the time we get in late Saturday night. At least when it rains we have barracks inspection and do not have to drill so we are able to get off earlier in the afternoon.

I am enclosing a picture of Bud MacFarland and myself that Mike Hardin, my bunk mate took. It didn't come out so bad. The building in the background is the gym and where some of the air cadet students live. Our barracks are to the right as we stand in the picture.

Don and Bud MacFarland
at the University of Tennessee

Now I'll try to answer some of the questions that you asked in the last letter. I'm not sure which "blue plane" that you mean as there are about three in the attic. The low wing army plane with yellow wings and a blue body should be worth about four or five dollars. The largest army bomber should be worth about four bucks. The large double wing navy plane should be worth about seven or eight dollars at least as it about the best job that I made. If you can sell any of the railroad you had better. The finished track should sell for about five cents a foot. If you can sell any more of it I'll send you the prices that I think you should get for it, Mother.

Did I say in my last letter that I had heard from Brant. The reason I had not heard from him was that he was sent to a star unit at Lincoln, Nebraska. He had been classified for Basic

term one but when the Basic program was discontinued, he was returned to Concordia. He said that most of the company was in Minnesota with PW's. Brant now works six hours on and twenty-fours hours off and is having and easy time in Concordia although he may be sent to Minnesota at any time.
I'll stop for Sunday dinner but will continue afterwards.

Ed Pyatt was taking engineering at Washington University, but he has since returned to the troops. He is now in the medics in an infantry division at Fort Lenard Wood, MO. Perhaps I'll be back in the army soon as we do not know anything definite.

I got a letter from Bud yesterday. His address is:

> Lt. C.B. Thatcher, Jr. 0-713620 18th Replacement Wing
> A.A.B. Salt Lake City, Utah

He said that he would be there for several weeks before he went into operational training on heavy bombers (B-17 or B-24). The greater part of his graduating class was sent to the east coast for training on medium bombers.

So Lew Kirchner was able to get a furlough. This will probably make him feel better when he returns to the army again. The armored forces are a tough outfit but they are not being used to much at present.

Have you heard from Mrs. Mikus that Ernie was to be sent to the armored forces Officers Candidates

Letter from Donald's friend Ernie Mikus

School at Fort Knox, Ky. That is three hundred miles from here but too far to go on a weekend.

We have finished the first six weeks of the course and I hope everything turns out all right. Most of us are worried about thermodynamics as the professor flunked sixteen out of seventeen in the civilian school. Here is hoping that I'll be able to get by.

Friday night we went to see an army show that was given to raise money for the Red Cross. It was very good and had some good army actors in it. I'll probably go skating this afternoon although I should stay here and study.

I'll close now and hope to hear from you soon.

Love,
Donald

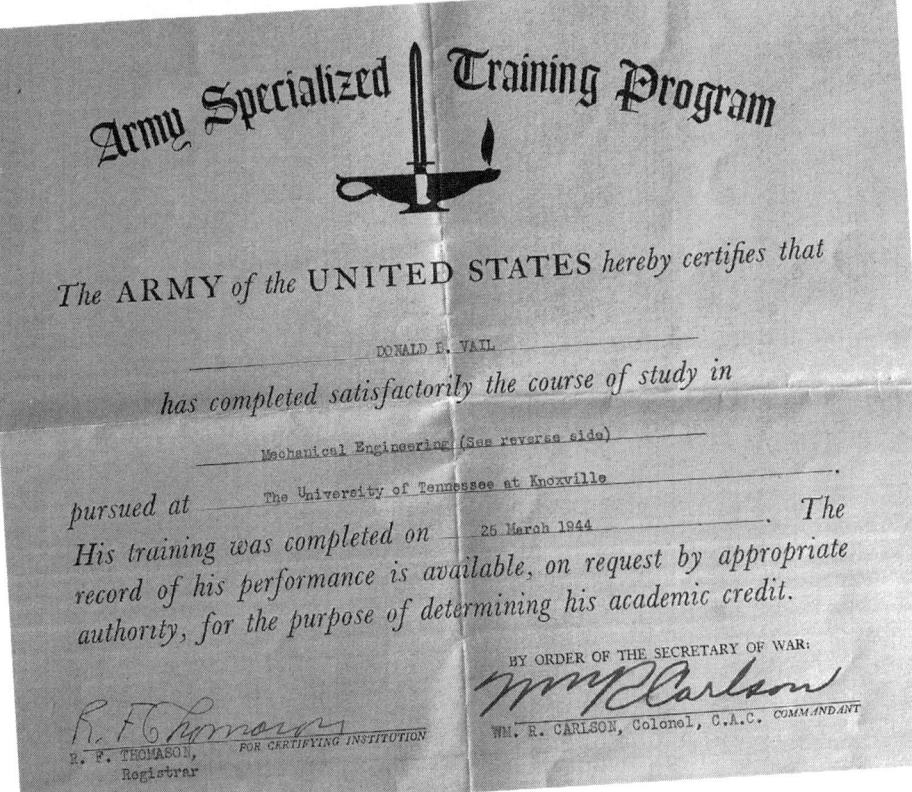

ASTP certificate of completion

Wenesday, March 27 [March 22], 1944
Univ. of Tenn., Knoxville, Tenn.

Dear Mother and Dad,
To begin this letter with a poem:
Our college days are over,
We won't get that degree
Put up that service flag, Mother,
They're closing the ASTP.

That is all there is to it. There were rumors ever since the beginning of the week to the effect that we would leave the halls of U-T. The rumors finally came true as shipping orders were posted in the day room this morning at eleven o'clock. Our group is to leave here early Saturday morning, as yet we are not sure of our destination.

We will probably go to the army replacement center at Camp Forrest, Tenn. This is a maneuver area. Most of the group is infantry that I am leaving with, but I will probably be put into the MP's again. I don't know what the address will be but I will write as soon as we arrive and are assigned to companies.

I'll send the books home as soon as I am able to get something to put them in. They all arrived some time ago. If I have time to read, I'll write and ask for them after I am located again.

Your letter arrived this morning telling me of your activities. Don't run down your health by working too hard and trying to do too much when you don't have to.

Don't worry about the sixty dollars. We won't be paid this month so you'll have to send me some money in a week or two.

I'll have my last date here in Knoxville tonight as I was able to get on the honor roll one week. If you're on the honor roll you were given an extra night off.

Oh, well, it was a lot of fun, but now it's back to work.

Love,
Donald

Infantry and Vehicle Maintenance Training

Camp Atterbury, Indiana

Camp Crowder, Missouri

Camp Rucker, Alabama

Altlanta Ordnance Depot, Georgia

Monday, March 26, 1944
Camp Atterbury Ind.

Dear Mother and Dad,

Here I am in the army again. We left Knoxville late Saturday night and spent the night trying to sleep on the train. We arrive in Louisville, Ky. on Sunday morning and as we had missed the early train, we spent about four hours eating and walking around. It is too bad I could make arrangements to see Ernie, if he was at Knox, but I don't have his address as yet.

After I wrote you last week we were told that our orders were changed. We were to be sent to Atterbury we our division was to be stationed. The 106th has just about finished with the Tennessee maneuvers will be shipped in here later this week. Just now there are very few soldiers in this camp as compared to the number that it can hold.

We are now stationed with the divisional headquarters company until the rest of the division arrives. We will then be assigned to the different companies. I don't know what chances I have of staying in the M.P.'s for it is quite possible that I may be assigned to the infantry with many of the other fellows. Other fellows from the ASTP are expected to be shipped here to fill up the division.

The 106th has a shoulder patch with a lion's head on it and it is know as the fighting lion division. I send you a patch as soon as I can get

The 106th's shoulder patch.

some. The division has been in training about a year and parts of it may be shipped out.

This is a fairly new camp and we have nothing to complain about after looking it over last night. Of course not everything is opened as yet. We were working the military police company helping to clean and set it up, but this was only detail work. We will probably be working K.P. and other details for the rest of the week as all of the buildings and kitchens need cleaning as they have not been occupied for a month or two.

It looks as if I'll have to ask for some money again. I spent most of the money I had left having a good time in Knoxville before we left there. We are fairly close to Indianapolis so I'll probably go in there on a weekend if we are able to get passes. We will probably be paid on the 10th of the month so I'll only ask for five dollars. If we don't get paid I'll send for more later. It won't cost as much to live as it did in Knoxville as we will be able to get everything at the PX.

I close now hoping to hear from you soon. The present address is on the envelop.

Love,
Donald

Sunday, April 2, 1944
Camp Atterbury Ind.

Dear Mother and Dad,

Well, here I am in the infantry. This is a far call from the MPEG's and ASTP. Time went fairly fast last week as we were doing a number of odd jobs until the whole division arrived. The final convoy came into camp last Thursday and most of the boys from U.of T. were assigned to companies that night.

Most of them were sent to one of the infantry regiments and no two in our small group were assigned to the same company. Several of the fellows were sent to the signal because of their knowledge of radio work. I and six other fellows from U-T were assigned to this regiment on Friday, but were sent to different companies. There were four other fellows in this company from U-T and later that day about twenty fellows from Vanderbilt and Alabama came in.

This is a rifle company, but I am now in the light machine gun section. We are to begin a review of basic training tomorrow. Most of this will be field work with what is known as dry fire. This means taking the different firing positions with the rifle. This outfit has M-1 (Garand) rifles so I'll have to learn all about this weapon as we had Enfield weapons in the 480th.

After the dry fire there will be a lot of range firing. Here is hoping that I can make some good scores as the competition will be good in this company and division. After the rifle we will fire different weapons in the company, probably carbine, pistols, mortar, and light machine gun.

I'll probably be able to get a furlough soon. Part of the division is leaving this week and some of the fellows from U-T are in this group. In this company the fellows who have not had a furlough in longest time will get theirs first. This will probably put me in the third group as the last time this company had furloughs was in December.

Tell uncle Roy if you see him that the 106th division was better than his 78th in the maneuvers. The unofficial opinion is that this was the best outfit on the maneuvers in Tennessee.

I have been attempting to catch up on mail this weekend. I still have a couple more to go. Did you get Ernie's new address for me? Did you send a letter to the divisional headquarters Company? If you did I hope that it will be able to follow me to this company. The mail has been all mixed up as none of the mail from the U. of T. has arrived yet.

I'll close now hoping to hear from and see you soon.

Love,
Donald

This is my permanent address
    PFC Donald B. Vail
    ASN 32923472 Co. C 422nd Inf Regt.
    APO 443 Camp Atterbury, Ind.

Saturday, April 8, 1944
Camp Atterbury, Ind.

Dear Mother and Dad,

I received your two letters this week. Thanks very much for sending me so much money. It finally turned out that I didn't need it as I was paid the day following the first letter. The money may come in handy if I can ever get a pass out of this camp.

At the present time my status is as mixed up as ever. Early this week all furloughs were cancelled and every one assigned to this company was given an overseas replacement furlough physical. Practical everyone passed and has been given a furlough except the noncoms. None of the ASTP men who were assigned to the company have been put on the replacement lists. There were a few of us who did not have infantry basic who were not checked or assigned to this company.

With only an attached status I am not able to send out laundry so I really have a pile of it. The rumors seem to have it that those of us who did not have infantry basic will be shipped to some camp where a thirteen week course will be given. I don't know how true it is but where there is smoke there is generally fire. Don't be surprised by another change to address.

With everyone out on furlough we have been pulling details one after another. I was on K.P. last Wenesday when the company had a beer party and it also turned out to be a farewell party for most of the private and PFC as they left on furlough that night. Tomorrow I am on K.P. again. With so many fellows on furloughs and a number of three days passes given out we could not get passes to Indianapolis. If we are here very long, I'll try to get home on a three day pass as train connections are pretty good to New Jersey.

The only other person besides myself in the machine gun section is the sergeant. This means that I have to fire the pistol instead of the carbine for record this week. In addition we have to fire the M-1 rifle for record and have been practicing positions all week. Monday we have to get up a three oclock to begin firing on the range at seven. You have not been in the army until you get in the infantry.

I still have the slide rule and a bunch of other stuff. I guess I'll have to mail most of it home as soon as I find out how. I have a Easter card but I don't have the stamps to mail it. You'll probably get it in a week or two.

Thank, Junior for buying the airplane, will you? I'll close now and will be hoping to hear from you soon.

Love,
Donald

Donald and some of his model airplanes

Monday, April 17, 1944
Camp Atterbury, Ind.

Dear Mother and Dad,

Well, I finally got a pass and it certainly was swell to see a city again. I began last week on Monday at three o'clock and generally got up about four. You certainly don't get much sleep around an infantry camp.

We got early as we were firing on the range. As all of the pistol men were on furlough I had to fire that weapon. We had to practice to do preliminary fire, and record fire all on the same day. It took a little while to get use to firing it again but it was all right after that. I qualified as a marksman as I could not hit rapid fire too well.

The following two days we were firing the M-1 rifle with a lot of waiting around in between. I was doing good with it as it is very easy to fire and hit the bull's eye. I had to go on guard one night with another company and it is the same old story. Wenesday the orders came in that unattached men were to leave soon. After I that we were put on all kinds of details to fill in time. I had K.P. on Friday and Saturday. We had to get up at three thirty and got off at nine oclock Friday and at seven on Saturday.

On Saturday night we were able to get passes to Indianapolis. We got into town about eight thirty and finally found a room to sleep in. After we got our bearing we saw several shows and went to bed.

On Sunday we walked around looking over the town. There is a tall memorial to the civil war which is really interesting. We spent several hours at the top and looking over the picture gallery. The collection on the civil war is excellent.

It looks as if the unattached men will be shipping out sometime this week. We are supposed to draw field equipment tonight or tomorrow. The rumors are fairly indefinite. Some of the fellows will go to Camp Crowder in the engineers. I don't know whether they will divide us up according to the military training that we had or will send us to another branch. I'd just as soon go into another section of the army other than the military police.

A long break occurred when I was issued the equipment. It looks as if we are prepared for any branch of the service.
I'll close now as it is getting late and I still haven't caught up with much sleep. I'll write as soon as I find out my next address.

Love,
Donald

An infantry patch of Donald's

Thursday, April 20, 1944
Camp Crowder, Mo.

Dear Mother and Dad,

I am just dropping you a line to get you know what happened since Monday. On Tuesday I began the day with K. P. as usual. During the morning we received orders to have our barracks bags packed and ready to ship.

The rumor that we would ship on Wenesday finally came true as we were assembled about eleven o'clock for shipment. Of course the men from our regiment had not eaten while the rest had. We finally got a chance to eat on the train. We saw the last of Indianapolis about three o'clock and made good time until we hit St. Louis about seven that night.

We got some good sleep as we had pullman cars so the traveling was pretty good as compared to most G.I. train trips. I had to pull the first hour guard on the mess car from 10 to 11 so that was all right with me.

We were up at six this morning for breakfast and finally arrived in Crowder a little while later. The trucks took us from the station to the battalion area where the major spoke to us.
He came out with the fact that we were to be with this company for only a short while as there was no place for us. He is really treating us fine as we have a place to sleep, eat, live, and able to have some cleaning done. I wish I could get some laundry done in one of these camps. He said that we would probably be shipped elsewhere next week as there are other engineer units here. This is mainly a signal corps post. I'm going to look up Bud McFarland tonight as he was sent directly here from Knoxville.

I don't know where or when we will be moving to next but we 150 fellows from ASTP are really seeing the country.

Write soon or wait a while until I'm settled.

Love,
Donald

Sunday, April 30, 1944
Camp Crowder Mo.

Dear Mother and Dad,

I received the letter that you sent to me at Atterbury last week. It was certainly nice to hear from home after several weeks. I also got the package of newspapers from you and it was a good thing that it did not have to travel any further. It had broken open but I received all of the papers. I mailed the slide rule and another package containing a bunch of winter clothing. Both packages are insured in case anything is broken or lost.

It looks as if I have forgotten another birthday. I know I am a little late I think but I send all of my best wishes and love, Mother. I'm glad to see that you were able to enjoy a trip to New York. Perhaps I'll be able to take you there if I am able to get a furlough with in a few months.

As you can see we are still here in Crowder. We have not done a thing since the second day we were here. We had to pull targets that day, since then we had only a few details as there are so many of us and we are assigned to one company and eat with others. I have played a lot of cards mostly bridge which I have learned as we have so much time with nothing to do.

After I had finished writing the letter to you last week I returned to the barracks and who should I see walking in the door but Ed Pyatt. It seems that he was transferred to this company from Fort Leonard Wood a week before. It was really swell to meet someone that I knew before. We went into Joplin last week but Indianapolis or Knoxville were a lot better for soldiers.

I went over to see Bud McFarland the other night. The electricals got a good break as they are going to school and will be able to get a rating when they are finished. About forty of our fellows were assigned to the battalion's line companies. After basic they will be transferred to H & S Company and be sent to schools for specialists training. Perhaps we will be able to get the same break when we leave here. At the present time the most of us left our air corps and MP's.

So far no orders have been sent in here as to what is to be done with us. All it will be is bridge until we leave here. I'll close now and hope to hear from you soon.

Love,
Donald

Friday, May 12, 1944
Camp Crowder Mo.

Dear Mother and Dad,

We are still here at camp Crowder and it looks as if we will still be here until next week at least. They are beginning to see that everyone keeps busy every day. Several warrant officers were made this week and one of them is taking care of us. Theoretically we are supposed to be taking training but we have been playing baseball all morning and afternoon out in the woods. Everyone including myself is as red as a beet from sunburn. The weather has become very warm after last weeks chilly winds. We will begin wearing suntans this weekend.

I see that you are wishing that I'll get a furlough. I am too, for I'd like to see home, again after all these months. It is practically impossible to get a furlough for quite a while yet. We can't get them while we are here and we won't get them after we get to another camp for some time. If the next outfit is in basic training, it will have to be completed before furloughs begin. If it is an old outfit we will be put on the end of the list of the regular men in the outfit.

I hope that you will be able to see Aunt Maude on Mother's Day, I know that you look forward to the trip to Edgewater. I was thinking that I would call you on Mother's Day but seeing that you may be out I'll call later in the week. I believe that you should get this letter Monday or early Tuesday. In any event I'll telephone you on Tuesday night as I think that you don't have to work that night, Mother. If anything should make it impossible for me to call on Tuesday, I'll call on Thursday night. I don't know how long it will take me to call to New Jersey, but I'll call as early as possible after seven o'clock. I think that you would rather have me do this then do anything else for Mother's Day.

Now to answer some of the questions were asked in the last letter. I received the box of candy just before I left Atterbury. We enjoyed it while we were cleaning rifles. I don't think that Ed and I will be able to stick together unless some of the rookics that they have in this battalion are shipped out instead of us. They would be giving us training if they were going to keep us here.

I'll close now and I will telephone you next week hoping to hear from you.

Love from your son,
Donald

Friday, May 19, 1944
Camp Rucker, Ala.

Dear Mother and Dad,

Well, it looks as if I have another permanent address for a while at least. We left Camp Crowder at 1 o'clock on Wenesday afternoon so I had to put in the call on Tuesday night. I didn't think anything about the election as I only read the headlines about Dewey and New Jersey, but I did not link the events together. I am happy that I was able to talk to Dad so that I could let you know what camp I was going to.

We went a hundered miles and stopped for about four hours at Springfield, Mo. to catch a train going South. In that time the hundered and five of us really took over the town and collected a number of addresses. One of the other fellows and I went to see a movie to kill time before we left. We went back to the train and found our bunks on the tourist car all made up.

The next morning, Thursday, we awoke in Memphis, Tenn. where picked up the train heading for Birmingham. We played bridge most of the day while we were riding thru Mississippi and Alabama. Most of the country is mountainous and we could feel it getting warmer and warmer as we got farther South.

We arrived in camp, which is down near the Georgia and Florida boarder, about 11 oclock last night. After we settled down for the night in one company, it was one o'clock. We got a physical check this morning and everyone was in perfect shape. You have to be half or more dead to get on sick call.

We were divided into two groups this afternoon. One group went to a treadway bridge company, a non combatant outfit, and the other went to a combat battalion. I am in this group. We will get a week's preliminary training when orders are completed. Tonight our group was told to which type of outfit we will be sent. I am to remain in this battalion although we have not been assigned to companies. Twenty-five of us will stay here while the rest are moved to other companies and battalions.

This is a new outfit formed about four months ago but we are the first men to be received other than the cadre (non-coms). The officer said today that he would keep everyone if possible, and that chances for readings would be excellent as we would have the jump on every one else who might come in. If fillers don't come in we might be able to get furloughs after a short time but it is impossible to count on anything as tentative as this.

Well, Mother, it looks as if we will have to make another date for a telephone call. Please let me know a good date and I will call then.

I'll close now and will write again soon.

Love,
Donald

Sunday, May 28, 1944
Camp Rucker, Ala.

Dear Mother and Dad,

Well, I have finally been assigned to a company. We were taking a week's course of engineer basic with a provisional company to help us learn some of the fundamental so that we might possibly become part of the cadre here to teach any of the rookies that they might receive. I doubt if we will get very many rookies in as another shipment of a ASTP men are expected by this battalion this week. After that we may receive some rookies or we may get more fellows who have had basic engineering in another camp.

I was interviewed by the captain in charge of plans and training last week. He said that some men would be sent out to the army ordinance depot at Atlanta, Ga. as long as I was interested and had studied mechanical engineering he would send in my name to be shipped there for the twelve week course. The course will cover the study of motors, so if I am sent I will probably become a mechanic.

The captain in charge of our company also interviewed us. He was interested in the fact that I had some drawing and some electrical experience. I don't know what it will all lead to, but I hope something good will turn up.

You said in your letter, Mother, that you would like to visit me down here. That would be swell, but there is not any towns to visit around this camp. This camp is poorly located if you want to visit with anyone. Perhaps if I am sent to Atlanta we will be able to make some arrangements so that you will be able to come down there to stay for a while. As things stand now I am about the fourth man to receive a furlough from this company. This doesn't mean much as by the time it will come up we will either start basic training or I will be sent away to school. In either case I won't be able to get a furlough.

I'm glad to see that you both have time to out in the fresh air and to pick up a sunburn as we have around here. Don't try to over do yourself as that won't help you in the least. I hope that Dad's garden is as beautiful as ever. I hope that have chance to see it sometime this summer.

Thanks for the long letter as it really helps me know what is going on in the rest of the family. How are Aunt Georg and Uncle Wes and their family these days?

Write when you have the time.

Love,
Donald

Saturday, June 3, 1944
Atlanta Ordance Depot Atlanta, Ga.

Dear Mother and Dad,

"A rolling stone gathers no moss", but I certainly am seeing the country and having a good time of it. I was the only one to be sent from the battalion back at Rucker as it looks as if I'll have to find some more friends. It seems that every time that I move I leave all of the fellows behind with whom I have been palling around. But of course I will be sent back to the 288th after I have completed this twelve week course. By that time I doubt if I'll remembered by more than one or two fellows.

I sent most of the past week on detail back at Rucker. All that you have to do is to move around and you will break out in sweat. A little exercise and some drill will really have the sweat pouring out of your skin. I am just as glad that I will not have to go thru basic training again because that outfit has a great deal of heavy work attached to it. It is necessary that you know a little about everything and there are a number of jobs.

Our company received twenty-five more fellows from ASTP this past week. They were in the infantry and were finally transferred to the engineers. I guess that they will be bucking for most of the line ratings.

We landed here in Atlanta early this morning after a sleepless night. The trains were crowded so I had to stand up for the greater part of the trip. Atlanta looks to be a fairly good city as there are plenty of people and a great many things to do during your time off. There is supposed to be a great deal of time off after the first week.

This is to a wheel vehicle automotive mechanic's course. This is about all that I have been able to find out so far. Tomorrow morning we to have some kind of meeting to tell us what everything is about. We will probably have to draw tools and manuals. I'll be able to tell you more about it later.

I'll close now as it is getting close to time for lights out. This should be a permanent address for the next twelve weeks so write when you have time.

Love,
Donald

Sunday, June 11, 1944
Atlanta Ord. Depot, Atlanta, Georgia

Dear Mother and Dad,

Two of your letters arrived this week and I think I should answer them now. When you wrote the last letter you had not received the letter from Atlanta. I guess I'll be able to straighten this mail situation in another week. I believe a number of people still think I'm at Atterbury, Crowder, or Rucker. It is rather difficult keeping up with everyone when I don't write consistently.

The school goes along pretty easy as there is nothing to the way to the method that they give tests around here. They give a short test everyday to see if you are awake. The mechanical work is a little more difficult as there is more to remember in order to have the unit to work correctly. Every thing as a different adjustment and it is only a matter of practice to work them out. Perhaps I'll be a mechanic after eleven more weeks. Who knows?

I received the first letter to Rucker that you asked about. The address should have been 1153 Eng. C. Group, which the larger unit to which engineer battalions and companies belong. This in turn is a part of the ninth corps, whose shoulder patch I wear. The ninth corps is a part of the second army for training purposes. I'll enclose a shoulder patch for your collection.

Mother if you wish to visit me down here, I guess it can be arranged.

We have a class B pass so that we may be out every night until 1 AM. We do not have to come in on Saturday nights. The best arrangement would be to come in near a weekend. Of course if you in attend to go to Florida it would quite a bit of time. It is about as far from here to Florida as it is from here to New York. Well, you can think about if you have the money.

Speaking of money you said that you were willing to send me some. I guess I'll have to take you up on that. With all the moving around last month I was unable to be put on any payroll so I was not payed. What are the possibilities of receiving around ten dollars? I'll get two months pay on the first of July but that is still three weeks off.

I'm sorry to hear that Norma was stricken with appendicitis just before graduation. I know she has missed a lot of fun. What happened to that card you were to send? I'll write to her instead.

So Arbor hit the big time again with the "World of Mirth". I should have liked to have seen it for I have not seen a carnival so a long time. There is supposed to be an amusement park near town so I think I'll see what it is like.

If I am going to write an more letters I'll have to finish this one. Write when you can.

Love,
Donald

Postcard post-marked June 13, 1944
Atlanta Ord. Depot
Atlanta, GA

Dear Mother,
In the letter I wrote yesterday I forgot to ask you to send me my swimming trunks. I send them home from Atterbury. Can you find them?
Your D-Day letter* arrived tonight. Don't worry too much about anything. Just keep going along. Don't work too hard

Love,
Donald

* See Appendix 1 to read a portion of Mother's D-Day letter

Sunday, June 18, 1944
Atlanta Ord. Depot, Atlanta, Ga.

Dear Mother and Dad,

I received your registered letter in the mail last night. It really came at the right time so that I did not have to borrow any money around here. I'll have to take it easy with my money until the end of the month when we will be paid again. There is plenty going on in the service club around here so it is just as easy to stay here for entertainment and much cheaper.

The school work is still going along fairly easily. We are now working on chassis and will be replacing units on the trucks all this week. Classes come in and out of here every two weeks and a group came in last night. The other barracks were all filled and fellows were sleeping on the floor, all unoccupied bed, and even outside on the grass. It all seemed very unusual when I came in after lights were out.

I am very sorry to hear about Aunt Maude. It is one of those things which must eventually come to those not in good health. Don't decide to spend too much of your time over there as it won't help the situation any.

Dad

This is Father's Day, Dad, so I will send you my special regards for this day. How is the garden coming? I imagine that you have as many vegetables this year as you do of flowers. Everything down here is in bloom as it would be in July or August at home. The temperature has been running about 95° in the shade and very much hotter out in the sun. I'm glad I'm not in Alabama as it was even hotter and more humid than around here.

It is time for Sunday dinner now as I am the only one in this squad room. I believe that we will have chicken, potatoes, ice cream, and other things. I am sure we will have string beans as they are on almost every menu. I expect them for breakfast one of these days. I hope we have ice tea as you know it is my favorite cool drink during the summer.

I'll close now as I have to dress before I eat. Write when you have the chance.

With all my love,
Donald

Sunday, June 25, 1944
Atlanta Ord. Depot, Atlanta, Ga.

Dear Mother and Dad,

Well, we have completed our third week on chassis and next Saturday we will be given our first monthly test. Last week we worked on the trucks replacing the different units, such as, the axels, steering gear, engine, transmission, and etc. This was interesting as this will be more of the actual work that I will probably be doing once I return to the engineers.

I noticed that you had scored different articles about army ordnance in the newspapers that you sent me. I hope that you have not gotten the idea that I am to be assigned to an ordinance company after I leave here just because this is an ordinance training center. I will be sent back to company B of the 288 Eng C. B. at Rucker or wherever they are sent.

The bathing suit arrived early this week so I have been able to go swimming. We generally hitch hike to a place about five or six miles from here, called Mirror Lake, out in the woods. It's really good as we can go swimming until 9:30 any evening. It has also been great to escape some of the unbearable heat of the afternoons. The heat makes it very hard to keep awake during any of the lectures. There are some swimming pools in town but they are generally crowded. Everyone has the same idea of attempting to keep cool for a while.

It seems that everyone decided to catch up with their mail this week as I think I got a letter from about everyone that I generally write to. Ed Pyatt was able to get the same break that I did, he was sent to dental technicians school, at Springfield, Mo. Bud Thatcher is training with his crew in Arizona but said that we will be hearing from him at another base. It would be swell if I could get to see him again.

I also got a letter from Norma telling me of her graduation. With all the letters I get, very few are from the same

Donald's cousin Norma Schlunsen

place so I am able to keep up with the rest of the country whether I've been there or not.

I'll close now as I should attempt to answer a few of these letters today as there is always something doing during the week. Write when you can.

Love,
Donald

Sunday, July 9, 1944
Atlanta Ord. Depot, Atlanta, Ga.

Dear Mother and Dad.

Five weeks have gone by already and time really flies around here. We finished the first week in the engine shop and I found this of greater interest than the chassis section. We tore down an engine and learned about the theory as we did so. We won't run the engine until next week but I'm sure it will sound okey. If I am able to remember more than half of the information passed out around here I ought to be able to make a mechanic.

Was Bud Thatcher able to get home before he flew out? I received a change of address card from him giving an A.P.O. number c/o Postmaster New York, New York. I guess that he will be flying over Europe before long. Soon the best meeting places for friends will be overseas.

Last night I was on guard duty and this was the best guard that I have ever been on. The ordnance training center posts all of the fellows who have to do any guarding at all. Civilians take care of most of this camp. The school battalion only furnishes a reserve guard for twelve hours and must stay in a barrack and sleep their time away. I wish I could pull all of my guard like this.

How do you like working in a servicemen's center? I have always wondered if the people who work in one are as interested as they seem. I hope that you are not working too much as I know that you like to go around and see things as much as I do, Mother. I suppose that you meet all types of fellows but that is the way that soldiers are.

The papers arrived this week and so I have been reading them today. It is really swell to learn what things of interest have happened at home. How did the 5th War Loan turn out and did you sell your quota of bonds?

Speaking of money I will get the rest of money for back-pay tomorrow. I'll get a money order and send it to you so I won't spend or lose it. You are able to spend twice as much money around here as you normally would in any regular army camp.

I'll close now so that I can answer some of the letters that are piling up around here. Most fellows keep up with their mail but it seems that I am always eight or nine letters behind.

Write when you have the time.

Love,
Donald

Thursday, July 20, 1944
Atlanta Ord. Depot, Atlanta, Ga.

Dear Mother and Dad,

Well, we have had two warm days in a row with rain at night and cool mornings. This has given me a chance to catch up with some of my letter writing at this time. Most of the time we go into town to a show, bowling, or swimming. Even if we don't go to town there is more doing at the Service Club than any two other camps that I have been in.

Last night all of the lights were out for several hours at suppertime. It turned out to be quite an interesting meal as I was told that I was getting Jell-O but it turned out to be beets. Any kind of a meal can be made up this way. I never did find out what the main course was.

We have completed more than six weeks now so we are heading into the homestretch. For this & next week we are conditioning a jeep engine that was in service for quite a while and then left to rust. I hope that it will run as well as the G. M. C. engine that we finished with last week. I like this work better than I did in the chassis department.

Your last letter arrived last Saturday when I was on K. P. I got the letter at one o'clock but did not get to read it until four. They really keep you moving in a large mess hall to keep you from gold bricking. I mopped the floors all day.

Our company back in Alabama is taking basic training and I'm glad that I am missing it. Another fellow was sent up here to this school and told me about it. The battalion finally got fillers from anti-aircraft and there are ratings in abundance back there. After basic a test will be given to determine who will keep their stripes and who will get them. I'll find out more about this later.

I'll close now as another fellow and I are going to walk to the service club to get some ice tea and cake.

Write when you have time.

Love,
Donald

Sunday, July 30, 1944
Atlanta Ord. Depot, Atlanta, Ga.

Dear Mother and Dad,

We have finished the first eight weeks of school with but four more to go. I hate to think of returning to Alabama. Perhaps by then my outfit will be preparing to move North. The battalion is now taking basic training but will probably move to some place rather North for maneuvers and field problems. Anything will be better than having to stay in Southern Alabama.

The test that we took on engines yesterday was more difficult than the previous tests as we were working on the "jeep" engine and the test was on the Dodge engine. Basically the engines are the same, but there are a number of minor differences. We also had a new instructor who was not too good. Tomorrow we moved to the third and last building for electrical circuits and carbeuration. This will be easy and you can learn a lot if you get a good instructor but many of them do not care as they have been teaching the subject so long and so often.

Your letter arrived yesterday noon and the newspapers last night. I also got a card from Aunt Bess and Uncle Pete from Glen Falls, N.J. I still have a stack of papers to read as I did not get up until late and I had washing to do before dinner. This afternoon another fellow and I went swimming in a pool in one of the parks in town. It was nice as the sun was warm as well as the water. On a whole the summer has not been as bad as you would expect. I thought that it was much worse in Alabama. The nights are cool so you can still get your sleep.

We are in the service men's center as you can see from the stationary, but will probably go back to the barracks or go to a show tonight.

Last Sunday another fellow and I went on a double date and went to a Baptist Church just outside of Atlanta. We had a nice time just as you would at home.

I hope that you are not working too hard at the Service Men's Center, Mother, because I know that they can become rather busy at times. Take things easy, Mother and Dad, and write when you can.

Love,
Donald

TELEGRAM Mother and Dad- Wire $100
Will call Sunday - - I have met the *one* *
    Love - Donald

Dear Harvey:
Don't have a stroke over the news. Please read the letter I have
written so that I can mail it tonight.
                     Honey.

* See Appendix 2 for Mother's first letter responding about "the one"

Thursday, August 10, 1944
Atlanta Ordnance Depot
Atlanta, Georgia

Dear Mother and Dad,

I think that this will be as difficult a letter to write home as any fellow must write. I know that you have had the telegram for some time and are wondering what has happened to me. To tell the whole story I have met the most wonderful girl that I have ever known and ever hope to know. We have been together continuously for the past few weeks so that I know her as well as I do myself.

I want to describe her and tell you a little about her so that you will get to know her and love her as I do. Her name is Paulette Iron and her home is in Oklahoma. I don't want you to think that Paulette is one of these pretty but flighty southern girls who do not have an ounce of sense. I know that she is able to cope with any problem and arrive at the best solution. We know that there are many problems to be faced and we are working them out together.

To describe Paulette, for she is as pretty as a picture, would be hard to do and the only way to appreciate her is to see and talk to her. Three of her grandparents were Spanish while the other was French. She takes her beauty from the Spainish side of the family as she has jet black hair, & a dark complexion. She is 5 feet tall, weighs one hundered pounds and has green-gray eyes.

Paulette has read the beginning of this letter which I wrote this afternoon. She says that I have not explained the situation and I know this to be true. It is impossible to describe any situation like this, but I must cover it to the best of my ability. I know, Mother, that you have probably had dreams of making plans for some fancy wedding but under the present circumstances, we wish to have a simple marriage ceremony before I return to Ala-bama. After I return there I should be able to get a furlough and we will be able to make the trip to New Jersey for our wedding trip.

Paulette will be eighteen next Friday we would like to be married on that date. I know that all of this has come as quite a shock to you both but I hope that you will understand and wish us the best of good luck and happiness that we desire. Mother and Dad, I want this marriage to be a success and I hope that you will share our happiness.

This letter will probably reach you by Sunday and will help to make you understand. We will telephone you collect in the afternoon so that it will reach you both.

until then

Love,
Donald*

Monday, August 28, 1944
Camp Rucker, Ala.

Dear Mother and Dad,

Well, here I am back in Alabama safe and sound, as well a single. We left Atlanta with memories of an easy life and good times on Saturday noon. Of course, with these high speed southern trains it only took us a day to go to the hundered-eighty miles. The train was an hour and a half late getting into Montgomery so we missed the train headed for Rucker and had to spend the evening in that town.

The last few days after we had finished carbeuretion we were working on a number of trucks that were out of com-mission. We had all these running after a few hours and gold bricked for the rest of the week. On Friday we received diplo-mas as having completed the course. I had K.P. on Thursday and I am glad that I'm finished with it in such a large mess hall. Of course I'd go on K.P. here tomorrow. It seems that the only sergeant that likes my work is the mess sergeant.

The training around here has been rough as there are hikes or physical training before breakfast and night problems or hikes several nights a week. The hikes are really going to hurt until after I can get used to them again. We are going to bivouac on Friday, Saturday, and Sunday. This is a lot different than Atlanta.

The furlough situation looks very good. At the present times there are about twelve fellows out on a furlough at one time for fifteen days. If I am put in the place where I should be I will be tenth on the list and should get one in about two weeks. I'll let you know more about it later.

I hope that you arrived home safely and with out an dif-ficulty in getting a berth. Let me know how you made out and how things are at home.

Love,
Donald

Sunday, Sept. 3, 1944
Camp Rucker, Ala.

Dear Mother and Dad,

This really is army life now. When I was in the infantry I thought that it was the toughest branch of the army, but now I have my doubts after the past few days and the schedule for the next few. I was able to take it easy on Monday and Tuesday as my barracks bags had not arrived and the company was having classes most of the time. Tuesday I was on K. P. and this is the easiest job around this company and it is no cinch.

On Wenesday we were preparing for Thursday with lectures and demonstration on air- ground liason. Thursday we went out in trucks to an area some fifty miles away. We were on the alert all day making contact with friendly aircraft and defending ourselves from strafing attacks from enemy pursuit ships. We reached the area about noon dug ourselves in and an eat our bag lunch. In the afternoon we worked on a road and then returned to camp under the same conditions.

We were up by five AM, as usual, and loaded everything on trucks for a tactical bivouac down on the Chatahowchee River on the Alabama-Georgia boarder. We set up camp about noon, ate, and our platoon received it orders. We had to return to Rucker Quartermaster area to get material for several bridges as well as assault boats. We loaded the twenty-five trucks and trailers by nine o'clock but I never got back to the area until two in the morning when we got something to eat. Eating and sleeping are not necessary while hard work is. Saturday morning we put up a pontoon bridge in four hours across the swiftest I have yet seen. In the afternoon we got a break in that we were able to return to camp on Saturday afternoon instead of today as it was scheduled.

I was road guard on, the way in an missed seeing the accident. A trailer on which a caterpillar tractor was hauled, turned over in front of the other company area. The three fellows riding on the "Cat" were lucky as they were thrown clear into the drill field and escaped with bruises.

You can imagine how warm you get when you work for
I am only writing a letter now an swet is dripping off my chin
and running down my chest. As our platoon did not work hard
yesterday afternoon we were given the job of unloading the
bridges when ever they got in camp. We fell out at one AM and
worked until four this morning. What an outfit!! Most of the
fellows are about my age nineteen, twenty, & twenty-one. The
non-coms are all in their twenties and no one cares about much
of anything. There are a number of fellows from anticraft who
have rating and they are losing their ratings so that about every
one is a private.

I should about number one on the furlough list but I don't
know when the next shipment will be. Several left on the 1st so
perhaps the next group will get theirs around the fifteenth. I'll
know better later.

Next week will even harder than the last. Monday there
are classes and physical training. Tuesday there is a physical
test which is really a killer including a four mile force march in
fourty-five minutes. I'll do my best but I am so far out of condition that I'll not be able to keep the pace up. For the balance of
the week there is another bivouac. If I seen anything in the past
week anything can and will happen.

Your letter was very interesting and I can see that you are
more observant than I am. I've seen so much of the country that
it all looks the same. From what I've seen this week the south is
even poorer than what you see from a train as we have been in
cotton raising country.

Thanks, very much, Mother, for sending Marion an orchid.
She said that orchids and roses are her favorite flower but I
should not have spent so much money.

Write when you can,

Love,
Donald

P.S. I received "Crazy Like a Fox" this morning. Also here is ten
dollar to cover the cost of the flowers. Don

Sunday, September 10, 1944
Camp Rucker, Ala.

Dear Mother and Dad,

I have finished one of the toughest weeks of physical punishment that I have had since I have been in the army. I have yet to find anything very soft about this outfit.

At least I have some good news. In the next three weeks this outfit begins training for the special job that you will hold in the company. Of course our regular training will continue with out let up. I begin working in the supply room tomorrow and I will hold the position of tool corporal for our platoon. Of course I will not get the rating of technician 5th Grade for sometime but at least, there is a good chance for it. This job is fairly easy as you must take care of all the tools that are in our chests instead of using them.

Last week was really rough. On Tuesday our company was given the honor (?) of representing the battalion in the physical fitness tests. Our company was the last to do the tests so it was plenty hot by the time we started. There were five exercises including several races any of which were enough to knock out a normal person. I was able to get thru these and take a fifteen minute break before starting the four mile forced march. The heat was terrific by this time and several officers had to fill in for fellows who had passed out. By the time we had reached two miles I was really on the ropes and an officer carried my rifle for the balance of the march. With out this weight I was able to keep in contact with the rest of the company.

On Wenesday we went on a bivouac to a park near Andalusia and this was terrific. We had to build a four mile road thru the park all day Thursday. It was a killer as it began raining in the afternoon so the swamps and streams did not bother us so much. It is not easy chopping trees, building bridges and road, and digging into the night. I think we had to haul every truck out of a mire at least two or three times. We worked Friday morning and then came Friday afternoon and a shower and dry clothes really looked good. They begin training us as night owls next week as there are two nights next week when we don't sleep. More roads to build.

I got your last letter on Friday so write when you get the chance.

Love,
Donald

Home on furlough with Mother

Oct. 4, 1944
USO postcard/Camp Rucker, Ala.

Dear Mother and Dad
    Just a line from Atlanta to tell you I arrived here safely.
I came down with Garren and several of the other boys. We
were only two hours late into here, but will still hit camp
tonight.

    Love,
    Donald

Sunday, October 8, 1944
Camp Rucker, Alabama

Dear Mother and Dad,

Well, I was able to get back to camp by Wednesday night without any trouble. We were only two hours late by the time that we reached Atlanta on Wednesday morning. We were able to catch the bus 20 minutes later and we're on our way back to Alabama. Bob Garren and I went back to Rucker by bus while the rest of the fellows returned by train later in the day.

A train trip back was not too bad except for the crowded trains. We did not have to stand although a number of people were. I found Garren went I went through the coaches and rode with him the rest of the way to camp. On the train from Washington to Atlanta we met a number of the other fellows from our company who had come down on the same train or on and earlier one. From then on the trip was pretty good as we talked over the furlough and everyone was willing to tell a better story than the next fellow.

Since we returned things have been running as usual. I had to fire the rifle on Friday for Record and made out all right. We also had a retreat parade that night after this a photograph took pictures of each company. I'll send one home as soon as I am able. I may send some clothes home sometime this week if I get around to it.

How did you and Aunt Emma and Roaul make out in New York? I hope that it did not rain all day. We hit rain in Trenton but the south was sunny. As soon as we hit Atlanta we were wishing we were in suntans instead of OD's.

Write when you have the time as I'll get the letter. I'll write again as soon as I have the chance.

Love,
Donald

Oct. 20, 1944
USO postcard/ c/o Postmaster New York, N. Y.

Dear Mother,

Just a short line to let you know that I arrived here okay after I saw you. As I told you the Christmas packages that you and Aunt Nete sent arrived yesterday. Last night and tonight I enjoyed opening the packages and everyone helped with eating the cake and candy. Thanks very much for everything even if it was an early Christmas. If you decide to send another package send cracker and cheese and other things to eat as they really hit the spot. Your letter has not arrived but I expect it tomorrow morning.
Write when you can.

With all my love
Donald

*See letter, Appendix 4, concerning Donald's deployment to Europe

Europe

England
France
Germany
Holland

October-November 1944
At sea

Dear Mother and Dad,

At the present time I am using an "at sea" address and you will not received this letter for some time after we arrive at our destination, where ever that may be. I'm happy to think that I was able to get home once before I departed, but I guess everyone wants a little more than he already has.

Our trip has been fairly pleasant as there are a number of different things to entertain you. This has been a good chance to catch up on your reading and sleeping. I have been able to read several books and magazines and the sea air makes you sleep well. During the day there is a short period of exercising on the deck. Perhaps if you are lucky and able to crowd in you are able to see a movie during the day. The movies are rather old and I have seen them I went again and saw "Gentleman Jim" and "Kiss the Boys Goodbye". We are also able to hear transcription of radio programs such as, Bob Hope, football games, and other programs. We even have our own musical request program. This afternoon boxing matches are being held on one of the decks.

All in all it has not been a bad trip. I have not been seasick yet but some of the fellows felt it when hit some high sea for a day or two. All is pretty calm this afternoon.

I bring this letter to a close hoping to hear from you soon. Incidentally I received the letter that you wrote the day that I was home.

Love,
Donald

Sunday, November 5, 1944
Somewhere in England

Dear Mother and Dad,

We have set up our camp somewhere in England but I'm afraid that it is going to take me some time to get use to the climate. I have yet to see a day in which the sun shone all the day. At the present time, it is raining fairly hard and everything has turned to mud. I am certainly glad that we have a roof over our heads and a warm dry place to sleep.

I have just finished eating dinner and it was very good. Here is the menu for dinner, steak, peas and carrots, mashed potatoes, relish, bread, and grapefruit juice. It hit the spot for as usual I did not get up for breakfast.

As yet I have not had much of a chance to see the countryside but will get a chance later on even if it is hiking on our own two feet. From what I have seen of the countryside it reminds me of the eastern part of Pennsylvania. The farm houses are old buildings made of stone and cement with slate roofs while some of the barns are thatch roofed. In the towns it seems quite unusual to me as every house is the same. Every building in one block is of the same type of construction while those in the next block may be similar or the same as the first. I'll be able to tell you more about the towns if we are able to get passes.

I suppose that it will be sometime before we are able to receive any mail but every one is after the mail clerk to make life miserable for him. I know that all of us are just as anxious to hear from home as you are to hear from us.

Today is also wash day. Everyone is digging out dirty clothes and going to work. All you see around the barrack is clothing drying. Everyone is looking for hot water, soap, and space to scrub. I guess I'll have to start to work after I finish a letter or two.

I'll be waiting to hear from you and Dad, Mother, with all of the news from home. We ought to be able to find out the results of the election some time this week. The boys were arguing all the time as to who should win. I'll write as soon as possible.

Love,
Donald

P. S. If you sent another package send any of the necessities that we will need. So far we have not found a place to buy soap, shaving cream, razor blades, playing cards (pinochle & straight) and cigarettes.   Donald

One of Donald's "Somewhere in England" letters

Somewhere in England
Wenesday, November 15, 1944

Dear Mother and Dad,

Mail is beginning to arrive again and I received my first letter from you dated November 3 on Sunday. Everyone feels much better seeing that they have again established contact with Home and I have been able to got news of the latest events there.

Since I wrote to you last I have been able to see some of England in the daylight as well as at night. We now use English money and are getting use to handling it so that we are able to know approximately the cost of each item. The people seem quite friendly however and appreciate our difficulties and generally lend us a hand if we should not understand their pronunciation or mistake the values.

I have been on pass several times and will probably go out tonight to another town we have not visited as yet.

On my first trip we went into a small town near here to get our first taste of English life. In order to get around the towns it is necessary to know your way or have a guide. Your nose is also another valueable asset. We wandered around until we found a fish & chips shop and they really tasted good. Later on we went to a dance with music by British soldiers band of three accordions, a drum, guitar, and piano. The dancing, as well as the music, was strictly American, however. After this we went to the TOC H which is this country's USO open to allied as well as British forces. There you can read, write, eat or anything else.

On another pass Bob Garren and myself went into Plymouth. We really had a good time seeing everything. We were able to get beds in the American Red Cross Hotel for two schilling (.40) then we could either eat there or another place in town that was still open. We really walked our feet off during the day time as we covered the city from one end to the other.

The view from above the harbor was excellent and well worth our trip to see the town from which the Pilgrims left for America. I would have liked to have seen Plymouth before the war in order to compare that with its present state. The wanton destruction by the ruthless Germans was terrible whether viewed by daylight or in the dark of night. It is a sight which is not easily forgotten. Even in this town we found the people are very friendly and willing to help us.

In the late afternoon we went to the cinema but we saw American films even though they were quite old. The people seemed to enjoy them as much as we did. One thing that was hard to get use to was smoking in the theaters. The smoke got thick after a while.

One thing I was surprised to see in the city was the double deck buses. They were very similar to the buses on Fifth Avenue, New York City. It is rather difficult to get use to the cars, trucks, & buses traveling on the left side of the road instead of right. It wouldn't be too hard for me to get use to England though, except for damp, rainy weather.

It is now a cold, Thursday morning. Last night we went into a town near here. At the Red Cross building we got coffee and sandwiches. They had two registers by states of fellows who had been there. There were three fellows from Dunellen. One had been in high school with me, and I have heard of another whose name was Mann. The third was Bob Burton. All were registered some time ago so there is little chance of meeting them.

I have to go to work now, so I'll have to close soon. We now have a PX but everything is rationed. So far I have not run short of any.

I'll try to get a money order today & send it to you. Write when you can.

Love,
Donald

Tuesday, Nov. 21, 1944
Somewhere in England

Dear Mother and Dad,

Time goes fairly fast around here and Thanksgiving is just around the corner again. From what I can find out we will have a good dinner on Thursday. Our cooks are preparing to put on a few extra men to cook turkey and what ever else happens to be on the menu.

I suppose by the time that you get this letter it will almost be Christmas time. I imagine, Mother, that you will be rushing around as much as usual attempting to complete your Christmas shopping just before the deadline. I hope that you will not try to do too much as you have in past years. I guess that you will have to do all of my Xmas shopping for me too.

I'll enclose a money order so that you will be able to do some for me. I wish that you would send Marion a dozen roses or if you can not get these delivered to her, at Christmas time, please get something that you think appropriate. Mail her one of the pictures that you have of me. Her address in case you do not have it is

Marion Dempster
43 Park Terrace
West Orange, N. J.

There ought to be a balance so I want you to buy a present for yourself as well as Dad. I hope this doesn't present too much of shopping problem. Thanks very much for this.

I'll close now hoping to hear from you soon.

Love,
Don

Tuesday, December 5, 1944
Somewhere in England

Dear Mother and Dad,

Tonight we had a pretty good mail call as quite a bit of old mail finally caught up with us. The letters dated as far back as October and the letter I received from you was dated the 10th of November. I also received the package that you mailed around that time. Thanks very much for everything. I also received mail from Miss Moore, Ernie, and Ed Cranch. Everyone received several letters so they are feeling pretty good tonight.

I just returned from the "Igloo Theater" a building where we generally see the movies. Tonight we saw our first USO show. It was really very good with its fine performers. The MC was excellent as an imitator, singer, and comedian. There was also a pair of singers who were good, and a drummer and pianist. All in all, it added quite a bit to our enjoyment.

I hope that you noticed my new title. Our promotions were put thru several days so I feel pretty good about that too. I still have the same job that I had in the states. I sent most of Sunday cutting off the old stripes and putting two pair of the new ones on.

The situation here is improving since things have gotten organized. We now have our on theater, PX, loud speaking system, and canteen. The canteen is run by the NAAFI (Navy, Army, Air Force Institute) a British organization but it is still supplied with food.

I'll close now hoping to hear from you soon.

Love,
Donald

Sat. Dec. 10, 1944
Somewhere in England
V-Mail *[Victory Mail]*

Dear Mother and Dad,

I have some time to spend writing letters so I got around to writing you again. The most interesting thing that happened to me lately was my trip to London. I was able to team up with Bob Garren so we had an excellent time seeing the city. We stayed in the Columbia Club, one of the numerous Red Cross Centers.

Attempting to see London is just as impossible as it would be in New York. Of course, we took a rubberneck tour of the city and were able to see the high spots. We saw Westminster, Buckingham Palace, Scotland Yard, Tower of London, London & Tower bridges, #10 Downing Street, Dicken's Old Curiosity Shop, Elizabethan houses, and other well known areas and places in the city. We were able to walk through St. Paul Cathedral and Westminster. High in dome of St. Pauls there is the Whispering Gallery. Here you can hear a father whisper his words toward a wall some 100 to 100 feet distance.

This cathedral and Westminster were the most impressive sites that I saw. I hope that I am able to make some future trip to London so that I'll be able to spend some time in these buildings. Westminster memorials and stones covering the famous people of England. In each of the cathedral were buried either states-man, soldiers, poets, scientist, or other famous people. It was very interesting to me as I know that it would be to you.

After the tour we spent some time looking around the shopping district and then the theater district. It was interesting to see the heart of the British Empire. The movies showed about nine-tenths American films as we saw "Casanova Brown." The plays were about evenly divided with Noel Coward having two, "Blithe Spirit" and "Private Lives of Elizabeth & Sussex".

This letter should arrive along with the Christmas rush so I'll wish both of you, Mother and Dad a very Merry Christmas, with hope that another Christmas will find us together again.

Love,
Donald

Tuesday, December 26, 1944
Somewhere in England
V-Mail

Dear Mother and Dad,

Here it is the day after Christmas and everything is back to normal. I spent most of the weekend in the barracks as there was not too much doing around here this weekend. On Saturday night I stayed here and several of us played cards for a while. Later on I opened the fruit cake from Mrs. Mikus and we had some cider from the canteen and this was the way I celebrated my birthday. We enjoyed the cake so all in all it was not too bad but I hope my next birthday will be under happier circumstances.

Sunday we did very little except welcome home some of the fellows who had been indulging in Christmas cheer. On Christmas the weather changed to a clear cold day so perhaps we will see some snow for New Year's. The dinner was very good as we had more than we could eat of turkey, potatoes, carrots, peas, cranberry sauce and everything else.

On Christmas night several of the other fellows in our platoon and myself went into a nearby town. About the only thing doing in town was a dance so we came in fairly early and very early considering the time that you would come in from town in the states.

I have been wondering whether you received my letter with the money order in it. Sometimes letters are fairly mixed up and seldom come in any sort of order. I hope that the allotment has been straightened out. November and December should be $25 each, but January will start a $45 allotment. I hope that everything comes out all right.

I received your letters of the eight and ninth as well as the birthday card before Christmas. Write when you can.

Love,
Donald

December 31, 1944
Somewhere in England
V-Mail

Dear Mother and Dad,

Well, here is the last letter of the year and I am very well, and everything has been okay. This is a very quiet New Year's eve as most of the fellows went into town. Of course, there are always a few fellows sitting around just talking and several of us writing letters.

Today was payday so every one feels pretty good with pay money in their pockets. Tomorrow I'll get a money order and can send some of the excess money to you. I suppose that it takes quite a while to get an air mail letter. We are still receiving Christmas mail and won't get the rest or last for some time. I am still wondering if you received the money order for Christmas. Check up on it if you can, it was for forty-four dollars.

I made an arrangement with one of the fellows who I have known for some time. You should receive a money order for sixty dollars from Mrs. Armen G. Boranian of Russellville, Ky. I loaned him the money to cover some debts so he will tell his wife to mail the money to you. I'm sure you'll get the money okay, as Armen has made me an offer of going into a partnership after the war. This sounds pretty good and we will have until we both finish college before we do anything definite. That would give us plenty of time before we make some good arrangement. Of course any thing can happen.

I'll close now as there is little new around here. I suppose we'll stay up until midnight just talking, smoking and even listening the radio. Almost all of the comforts of home, but now a card game has started.

Write when you can.

Love,
Donald

Sunday, January 7, 1944 *[1945 Ed.]*
Somewhere in England

Dear Mother and Dad,

Well, another week has passed and everything has returned to normal after Christmas. Actually we had our biggest Christmas mail on January 5th for that was when the greatest number of packages arrived. Everyone had at least one or two packages although most of them had been received at an earlier date. We also received most of our Christmas cards in the same mail so we a number of things to open, read, and eat.

We have sent most of the weekend eating from these packages rather than going to Chow. Everyone has something in their duffel bag to eat. I received the package that you mailed containing soap, razor blades, and shaving cream. Thanks very much but at the present time we are able to get these articles thru the ration system at our PX. The package that the church mailed also arrived and contained a number of things to eat.

It is pretty much like home around here tonight. We have the radio and are listening to a re- broadcast of Jack Benny's program. It seems like Sunday at home with this and everyone sitting around just reading or writing letters.

I received the V-mail letter that you wrote on Christmas night. That is one night that I would really like to be home in every year just to enjoy the fun of opening presents and seeing every one. Too bad that not everyone was able to attend. I'm glad that you received the money order in time to purchase the Christmas gifts for you, Dad, and Marion. Thanks for taking care of every thing.

I am enclosing a money order for $36.00 and put this away in one of the banks for me, if you please. Every thing has been quiet around here so I'll close now.

Write when you can.

Love,
Donald

January 20, 1945
Saturday Somewhere in England
V-Mail

Dear Mother and Dad,

This is the end of another week and so here I am. We had a heavy snow during last night and it was almost like some of the snow storms at home. Usually there are only light flurry with the snow falling in compact balls rather than the heavy flakes, but last night, we had flakes instead. It was quite pretty to see it stick to the boughs of the trees.

I received a letter from Ernie this week. It was one that he had written when he was home just before Christmas. I hope that he was able to get home for Christmas.

Our courses that we are to take during our spring time (none too much) arrived this week. Mine on diesel engines seems very good there are about nineteen lessons but I have a good background for many of the lessons so most of them will not be too difficult.

Pamphlet about the Corps of Engineers

Perhaps you noticed in Stimpson's report what happened to the infantry division that I was in for awhile. I am certainly glad that I got into the engineers now.

Write when you can and I will do the same.

Love,
Donald

Monday, Feb. 5, 1945
Somewhere in England

Dear Mother and Dad,

Here I am again after some time. As you can see we have
moved from our new address. Our quarters are much improved
since we left the Nieson huts and barracks. Now we have many
of the improvements of a modern residence. We now have
rooms in which four of us sleep so it might even be called semi-
private rooms.

As usual very few of England's houses are centrally heated
so each room has its own fireplace. There are three of us writing
letters at our table next to the fire. I am sure that you'd enjoy a
fire place, Mother, but it is necessary to burn too much coal in
order to heat even a small room.

We went into town yesterday and really had a swell time.
We walked all around the town in order to get our bearings
and to locate different places where we might spend some time.
Later we went to the amusement pier and enjoyed ourselves riding on the different rides. It was a lot of fun. There are a number
of places where you can go.

We found a theater where different stage shows are put
on. This week one of Noel Coward's plays is being put on. If I
can get another fellow to go I would like to see it one night this
week.

Last night we went to hear a concert given at the large
ball-room. There was a Negro band (civilian) that was excellent. They played all the well know swing and novelty tune all of
which were American. There is very little music in the popular
vein which is originated in England. For the rest of the week
this band will play dance music so it will really seem like home.

Incidentally we had the first ice cream sundaes that I have
had since we left the states. In order to take up for lost time we
each ate four of them.

I am enclosing a money order for fifty-dollars to be added
to the bank account or for what ever you may need it. My in-

creasement in the allotment should take affect with the February check as it takes some time for them to catch up with every thing.

I received the box of Christmas gifts that you sent from Aunt Ida & Uncle Roy and Aunt Gladys and Uncle Russell. Thank them for me if you should see them before my V-mail reaches them. I'll write to them later this week.

Ed Pyatt sent me a letter this week. He said that he was making out all right and that he is now in Luxembourg. I hope that he makes out all right. Miss Moore's letter said that Bud would probably be started for home sometime this month. Perhaps I should have joined the air corps too.

I'll close now hoping to hear from you soon.

Love,
Donald

Feb. 19, 1944 [1945]
England

Dear Mother and Dad,

I am writing this letter from the American Red Cross several blocks from our building this Sunday. It is rather noisey with a radio playing, people talking & eating and other playing ping pong. I suppose I'll have more trouble with people sitting down next to me and talking to me, but perhaps I'll be able to finish this and perhaps another.

Some of the back mail caught up with us this week. I have received both packages now and thanks for sending everything. Mother you had better thank everyone who has sent me something as there is generally not enough time to write to everyone that I really owe letters too, also you know me and letter writing. Thank Mrs. Mikus for sending the food as we have been eating it at night and it really hits the spot. We also have a chance to buy cake and pastry in the bakery next to the Red Cross.

I also received a letter and the valentine from you. Incidentally you did not say whether the pet was a puppy or a kitten. It sounded more like a puppy in the note. Teddy sounds like a pretty good name for him although you will probably have a definite name for him by this time.

Uncle Roy wrote from Tennessee and Aunt Ida from home. I should write to them tonight as long as I don't spend too much time on any one letter tonight.

Marion wrote and told me that she received the roses and pictures. I imagine that she has written to you thanking you for the trouble that you went to obtain them for me. I certainly will be glad when I'll be able to spend a Christmas at home.

This week went by pretty rapidly as we were kept pretty busy. There were two dance given this week. The battalion gave a dance one night with the battalion dance band furnishing the music and the town furnishing the dates. The company dance was much of a success with the same dance band and with only fellows from our company present. The jitterbug contest was interesting with one of the fellows from our platoon winning with a girl who was the date of another one of our boys. Nearly everyone in the company showed up at one time or another.

I'll close now so that I can write several more letters. Write when you can.

Love,
Donald

P. S. I'll enclose a request for the newspaper I request that the "Plainfield Courier News" be sent to my overseas address
Cpl. Donald B.Vail 32923472 Co. B 288th Engr. C. Bn
APO 508 c/o Postmaster New York, N. Y.

Sunday, Feb. 25, 1945
Somewhere in France
V-Mail

Dear Mother and Dad,

Well, here I am again, but this time writing by flashlight in a tent in France. It is night and very little to do except talk, sleep, or write if you can obtain enough light. Tonight the loud speaker system is playing records to make it more like home.

We arrived here after a very smooth crossing of the Channel. I guess that we were fortunate as the weather is generally rough during this period. France is much more like the United States in its countryside than England. England has everything cut into small sections by hedgerows but France numerous hills, valleys, and streams. There are many farms and small villages and we were glad to see that the farmers were beginning to till the land and in some places were planting hot house cuttings of hardy plants. This means that spring can not be too far behind. The weather has been pleasant as the sun is warm during the day, but the nights are chilly even with several blankets and a bed roll.

We are now writing by candle light and sitting next to our wood fire. With a wood fire it generally takes part of your day cutting wood with which to keep warm at night.

I received the letter that you wrote on Jan. 15th. From now on money is not of much use or value. There is very little chance to spend it except for candy and cigarette ration or for "Stars and Stripes", the army newspaper. The paper here in France is much than the London edition as it gives a more complete coverage of the news.

In the letter you wished to know how much to charge Junior for the table. I guess that about ten dollars would be a fair price as I only have a rough idea of how much it actually cost. If that was a Lionel switch that you sold it would probably sell for two or three dollars.

I'll close now hoping to hear from you soon.

Love,
Donald

Sunday, March 11, 1945
Somewhere in Germany
V-Mail

Dear Mother and Dad,

Another week has rolled around and I again have a chance to drop you a line. I received two letters one from January and the other of Feb. 6th. It seems to take longer and longer to receive letters from home. Of course it is also taking more time for me to write answers. Tonight several of us are writing by candle light in the kitchen of an old German inn.

As I used to say when I wrote in the states that you really get around. I have been in Belgium and Holland, as well as here. It is rather difficult attempting to keep one's money straight, but then there is little use for money here.

I was glad to hear that Bud was home. Did you get to see him? Send me his new address as I have not heard from him in some time. I received a letter from Ralph and I'll look him up as soon as I can locate his outfit.

Write when you can.

Love,
Donald

Tuesday, March 20, 1945
Somewhere in Holland
V-Mail

Dear Mother and Dad,

I received your letter of March 5 in the past few days and this was quite rapid service. Sometimes mail gets to us anywhere from three to four weeks late, I suppose that mail headed the other way is the same. By the time that you receive one letter it seems that I am in a different place from where I wrote the previous one.

So they now have Lew over here. Chances are slight that I will meet any of them around here, with the exception of Ralph if I am able to meet. The only way would be to get a pass at the same time he does and that would be doubtful, I have not heard from Ernie since I was in England and he wrote from the boat. I received a short letter from Ed but he says, as little to say as I do about anything definite.

I am glad to see that you are able to read so many books. We read our newspaper, Stars and Stripes & Yank, but we don't have time for much more. I have been able to play a couple of games of chess. It is surprising how much one forgets in a short time.

Bob Garren gave me a hair cut this afternoon. I had my hair cut short again as it much easier to keep clean & neat.

Tonight I am writing by the light of a gasoline lamp from our large tent. We have more room here than we had in the buildings. Several Brit-

Corporal Teddy

ish soldiers were visiting us and attempting to make a trade for American wrist watches. No go tonight.

I notice that you intend to send a package. Only send food as this thing that we run short on between meals.

Corporal Teddy must be quite playful and keep you interested. I imagine that you are going to have trouble with a 12 o'clock ruling. I suppose that Dad will be working in the garden. Spring is just about here as the trees are budding and the weather as been clear.

I received a letter from Bud, from Atlantic City. It seems that he had quite a time on his furlough. I wish I had been there at the same time.

Will write more later.

Love,
Donald

Friday, March 30, 1945
Somewhere in Holland
V-Mail

Dear Mother and Dad,

Here I am again and still here in Holland. The weather is fairly good as spring will soon be in full operation. In some places that I saw today there were daffodils, hyacinths, and the yellow bushes that grow in the yard. It seemed more like home.

We went into a city for showers today. It felt good to get a hot shower. The other time I took a dip in the pool, but it was too cold to stay in very long. The town is in fair condition with numerous civilians which is unusual as the small towns are empty.

Several of us saw "Double Indemnity" at the Naafi cinema. It was a good show and we enjoyed it. The Canadian newsreel showed a picture of the circle just outside of the building in which we saw the picture.

Incidentally air mail is getting here quite rapidly. I received your letter acknowledging that I was in France.

Write when you can.

Love,
Donald

Wednesday, April 4, 1945
Somewhere in Germany

Dear Mother and Dad,

I'll write a line or two while I'm waiting for my hard boiled eggs to cool. Tonight everyone is cooking their's to suit themselves instead of eating them the G.I. way (scrambled).

They where really good and hit the spot. Fresh eggs are much better than powdered or frosten. There are even some benefits to being in Germany.

I received your letter tonight dated March 20 so the air mail service isn't too bad these days. It was too bad that Niggy was poisoned and I hope that nothing happens to the puppy. I am sure that Corporal Ted is cute even though he is attempting to tear up everything in the house.

I'm glad that you received a letter from Armen's wife. I'm sure that she is very nice even though I have never met her. I'm sure she would appreciate a gift for the baby.

Speaking of gifts it will be about time for your birthday, Mother. I'll have to wish you happy birthday from a long ways off. I wish that you would purchase yourself a gift from the money that I have sent home and from the money that you can get from Junior. We don't get paid any too often, but it doesn't make too much difference as there is little chance to spend it.

The scenery here in Germany is somewhat like southern New Jersey in some parts but in some parts it is none to pleasant even yet. The Rhine did not impress me as much of a river even though it is rather swift.

I'll leave you now to hit the hay. Write when you can.

Love,
Don

Tuesday, April 17, 1945
Somewhere in Germany
V- Mail

Dear Mother and Dad,

I hope that you had a happy birthday, Mother, and that you will have many more. I suppose that I will hear how you spent this birthday in several days. I hope the weather was pleasant at home as it is around here.

I suppose that you were able to guess that we were with the 9th army for a while. We did not actually work for the 9th as we were doing work for the British after our first assignment.
The places were quite torn up along the line where the winter was spent. In that area Germany was really smashed to bits as there were numerous towns cities and the English took towns slowly and methodically. The Americans take areas by smashing it and then gaining rapidly.

I have seen many places of interest and that have made the news, but I did not see them at the same time.

I'll write more later.

Love,
Donald*

* See Appendix 5 for a portion of Mother's letter following the death of Presdent Roosevelt

Monday, May 7, 1945
Somewhere in Germany with the 15th Army

Dear Mother and Dad,

Today is the day to which we have looked forward to for sometime. This is V.E. day. I suppose this means much more to you at home then it actually means to us. To us nothing seems different except for the fact that all of us are a little relieved and greatful that this war is kaputt (finished), as they would say in Germany. Probably there will be a big celebration and I am sure that we would really like to see it.

Today is the first day of sunshine in the past two weeks. I think that we have been as cold or damp as any time during the winter. Spring should really be here to stay. All of the apple and cherry blossoms are falling from the trees but every thing else is a bright green. All of hills surrounding us are in the height of spring time.

Our living conditions are pretty good now as we have electric lights, tables, and a good mess hall near our school house. This is almost like working at a regular job as we had Saturday afternoon and Sunday off as the German workmen did not work. It isn't a bad life after all.

How did you celebrate your birthday, Mother? I hope that you had a swell time no matter what you did. By the time that this letter gets home it will be time for Dad's birthday. Happy birthday, Dad, and the best wishes of the day.

What type of present did I give you, Mother? I wish that you would get one for dad that would be just as useful. Incidentally we ought to be caught up with our pay this month. Perhaps one of these days I'll be home so the we can celebrate Dad's birthday with a strawberry short cake once more.

Mother I wonder if you would mind doing me another favor. I wish that you would send Marion a dozen roses on May 28th. I hope that this letter doesn't take too long in getting home so that you will have enough time to accomplish this.

I received a letter from Ernie while he was in Belgium. I guess he is out of the armored force now as he said that he wanted to get into Military Government. I don't think that it will be too difficult for him now that the war is over.

I'll close now hoping to receive your latest letter in tonights mail call.

Love,
Donald

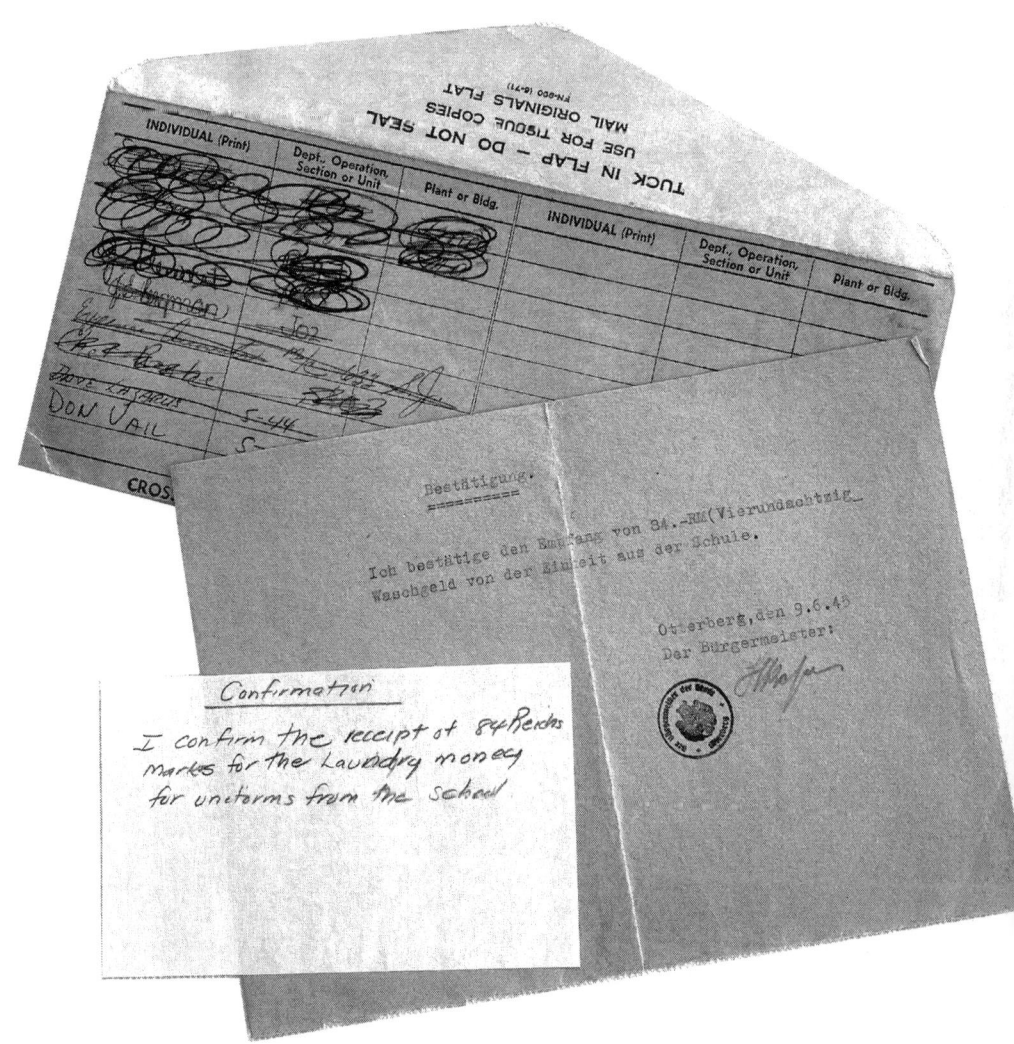

Records of laundry done by the German women

Thursday, May 24, 1945
Somewhere in Germany with the U.S. 15th Army

Dear Mother and Dad,

Well, with the completion of the war everything is just about returning to normal. This will be the first letter that I have sealed since we left the states back in October. I hope that I don't cut my tongue sealing the envelope as several of the fellows have done.

Mother and Corporal Teddy

We have a pretty good job now for our platoon. We are away from the company so it makes a little more work for me concerning supplies and laundry but it is still easy enough.

This afternoon I am writing from the large room which serves as combination supply and living quarters. There is plenty of room and light as this was a school house before the war. It is a little chilly today as it is cloudy and has rained a little for the last two days. When the sun is out this town in the valley really warms up.

This afternoon I am collecting the laundry that is done by the German civilian women. They do a very good job for us as everything comes back snow white and well pressed. This is the cheapest laundry that I have ever had to pay for. We are able to send out a half a barracks bag for one and a half Marks ($.15) and half a bar of G. I. soap. The women come here one morning as early as 5:30 when I issue it at 7:00 or 7:30 and deliver it that night or the next day, as today. I believe that the main reason that they take it is to get the soap as they are willing to take any number as long as they get the soap.

All of the other fellows are out working now. A few are in the back yard nailing and I can hear the saw cutting in the near by saw mill so the fellows over there are making beds. Other fellows are out making deliveries or picking up lumber. It is quite interesting and you get to see the surrounding territory.

The other night we went into the nearby large town and saw "A Tree Grows in Brooklyn." It was pretty good I thought and follows the book quite faithfully. We will probably see some entertainment around here now. We went into another town Saturday with me driving and saw a special service show put on by French entertainers. It was very good with its American M. C.

I received your last letter with a picture of Mother and Cpl. Ted. It is interesting to see him after hearing so much about him, he must be very cute. Incidentally we got our dog back after two or three weeks. He is a large German police dog named Max and a good guard to have with you. I think some civilians had him but he must like G.I. chow much better.

I suppose that you have seen the point system back in the states in the newspapers. I have a total 40 points after every thing has been totaled. It looks as if I will be here a long time with more than twice that needed to get out of the army. I still have a chance to get more of an education as information is beginning to be circulated on the educational system for the troops here on the continent. I think several universities here as well as the British Isles will be used as it would not be too bad if they are offering courses that are in my line. One never knows what will happen next.

The next time I write I'll tell you more about the different places that we have seen and where we have been. We really got around as this place is relatively small in comparison to the states.

Will you please have the "Courier" change the address to APO 103. Thank you. I'll close now and write another letter or two.

Love,
Donald

Sunday, June 10, 1945
Somewhere in Germany

Dear Mother and Dad,

Well, here I am again. We have returned to the company after living away from them for some time. We really had a good time and put in some hard work along with it. For this work we received a recommendation and are to receive three days off beginning today.

I don't know how much I'll be able to write as we are waiting around for everyone to get ready to go visiting. We are going over the Rhine to visit Heidelberg. I hear that it is interesting but I will tell you more about it after I return tonight.

Lately I have received your latest letters and some that were addressed to older APO's. I am receiving the newspaper quite regularly and is only about three week old although a back issue straggles in once in a while.

While we were in the area near Kaiserslautern we had a good deal from the army. We made deliveries to a number of Displaced Persons Centers in the area. We visited towns which were really destroyed by the war. Saarbrucken and Kaiserslautern were both torn up from one end to the other. When you come down a hill overlooking the town it seems as if a town were a saucer. The center is really about flat while many of the residences around the town are still standing. At present the major industry of most town is the restoring of public utilities and clearing and rebuilding the cities. Of course small village still are at their main occupation, farming.

It must be interesting work for you, Mother, working in the telephone exchange. I suppose that there are large numbers of soldiers coming into the states instead of leaving as formerly. Some of our fellows have left for the states under the point system so you might accidentally run into one of them.

The pictures of Cpl. Ted were very good from what you say he must be full of the devil and he looks it. The pictures of you and Dad were good see as well as the group picture of the gang on Easter Sunday. I can still name everyone in the picture.

(A change in pens used at this point. Ed.)

It is twenty-four hours later and we a reciting some of the tales to the rest of the fellows. We really had a swell time and spent the whole day sight seeing.

We left here in time to arrive in Heidelberg about twelve o'clock in order to eat at the transit mess hall. This was former-ly a restaurant. We were served by French girl and listened to a French swing orchestra, all girls. We then walked around town but all the stores are closed on Sunday and finally went to the Red Cross for coffee and donuts and to find out what was do-ing. Several of the fellows went out walking through the town, another to the symphony orchestra concert which was excel-lent I was told, while two other fellows and myself went to tour the castle.

The castle was a marvelous structure with its fine terraced gardens and deep moat. As you can see from some of the cards I am sending some of the buildings were knocked downed by the French in the 1700's. Parts of the castle were built over 500 years ago and the last in the 1200's. Several of the buildings were recreated for repainted but the buildings and sculptures in the original were excellent. The rooms were beautiful with their inlaid wood and paintings, but most of the furniture had been removed. The chapel, the original, was orate with its statues and decorations. We also saw the wine cellars and were fasti-nated with the size of the casks. The smaller held 10,000 gallons, 60,000 bottles, while the larger of the two held 49,000 gallons or 300,000 bottles. A pipe lead from the cask to pantry above which served the King's hall. Incidentally the casks have not been filled since 1769 but are empty. It was well worth the time we spent there.

After this we rode around town looking at everything. Nothing was damaged in the town as it was never bombed. We eat chow and headed back with intentions of seeing a movie in some town. When we got to Manheim we went to look up a theater and found out that there was a stage show by the French so we're headed for that. This show was much very better than that which I saw before. They spoke in English so more comedy was available. We decided to make a day of it and waited to see a movie but this was very poor and we finally got home at twelve o'clock.

We saw the Ernie Pyle Memorial bridge, mainly for railroad traffic, and several other bridges. I walked other the Roosevelt Memorial Bridge some time ago and it was the best fixed bridge that I have seen.

This morning I was routed out of bed to see the C. O. I was informed that I was to change jobs. Now I will moved into the supply room as armorer but at the same rating. The job will be a little easier but with more paper work. The only thing that I don't like will be leaving the fellows with whom I have been with for almost a year.

Well that is all the news for now and will close hoping to hear from you soon.

Love,
Donald

Tuesday, July 24, 1945
Germany

Dear Mother and Dad,

Well, here I am again with a much belated letter. Since I have been working as armored I have been kept quite busy during the daytime and often at night. Of course this is no excuse for not writing.

After I had been working in the supply room for a week or so, the supply sergeant, Dave Erlandson, was able to get a pass to Paris. From what I have been told, that is really a beautifully city, and is even better than London. It was unfortunate that I was too far down on the list to be able to get a pass to either Paris, or even Brussels, another interesting city. I don't know whether I'll have the chance to visit either city, now that we moved.

I really had a lot of fun, and trouble, running the supply room. Everything has worked out all right though. About the time that we were able to get everything running smoothly again, the French began occuping the Palitinade area of Germany. This necessitated our long trip about Germany.

We left Pfeddersheim, a few miles west of Worms, early Wednesday morning two weeks ago. From Worms we travel to Mainz in our 6 ton truck and trailer with bull dozer. At Mainz the battalion convoy passed us and it began to rain. We slept on top of our load until we were on the auto bahn (a highway similar to Route 29) from Frankfurt to Kassel. We arrived in the area of Melsungen a few miles south of Kassel and got lost as we were on the wrong side of the river and the bridge had not been completed. We finally got back to the company and were informed that we would bivouac in the pine woods. It seems that our order had been changed from the seventh army to the third army for some reason. It felt pretty good living in the open again even if it did rain two nights. It was pretty good, in that all we had to do was eat chicken every day and play baseball.

When our order came thru we found that we had a two day trip into Southern Germany. The weather was bright and sunny and we rode out-side the truck so that we could see the scenery and I ended up with a sunburnt face.

We rode to Auto-bahn back to Frankfurt, but only went thru the out-skirts of the city and finally back to Manheim on the Rhine where we went to draw our supplies previously. From Manheim we went past Heidelberg where we could see the castle in the distance, down to Karlsruhe, where we turned to head east toward Munich. We bivouacked that night on the Auto bahn after reaching the site before the convoy which was a feat for heavy vehicles.

The next day we traveled thru some of the beautiful parts of the Bavarian Alps. It was mountainous but we still made good time until the heat cracked one of the tires. After an hour or so of work we were dirty and hot so we decided to swim in the next river. We found a small lake and swam for a while before pro-ceeding. We finally arrived in another bivouac area near Augs-burg in time for chow. After several days we finally were able to start for Munich and the city of Freising, where we now live.

We were ahead of the convoy. As we entered Munich, we ran into difficulties. We followed the convoy route and ran into a low railway bridge. This damaged the bulldozer, but of course this did not bother the truck in the least. We transferred to another truck and went on.

Munich, from what we could see, was really a beautiful city before the war, but of course it was severely damaged by bomb-ing. Even now you need a pass or official business to visit the city. I'd like to see all of it.

We arrived at our new residence early in the evening, and by night fall we were operating at full speed again. We have plenty of business but every once in a while things slacken up a bit. I'll tell you more about this town and what we have to do, in my next letter.

It is getting rather late so I'll close now hoping that I'll hear from you as soon as we begin receiving mail again.

Love,
Donald

Stateside

Donald returns from Europe

October 1945
Washington, D. C.
(Fort Belvoir, VA. return address on envelope)

Dear Mother and Dad,

Well, here I am in Washington. I arrived in town Thursday evening about 6.30 so it almost took four hours to get here. The trip was not bad as I had a seat all of the way down. I had supper and walked around for a while before I took the nine o'clock Seaboard train down to Belvoir. We had to check into a number of buildings before we were finally assigned to a barracks. It was all right though as a truck picked us up at the station and carted us a round.

The next morning I ran into one of the fellows from B Company of the 288th. I was surprised to learn that there were about twenty or twenty-five of us here in the battalion. I have met quite a few of them wandering around. Of course, a few of them will be getting out with in a week's time as they have over seventy points. Those with sixty points will be getting out some time next month. They are discharging a few from this camp each day but they also are sending a number of the separation centers.

The company and battalion to which I am presently attached is only a processing outfit. Here they check your record, qualifications, points, and clothing as well as interview you. It takes about a week and then you are transferred to another battalion in this camp.

I was able to get a weekend pass this afternoon and come into town. I did not head for any place specially just wandered around. I went into the building containing the National Archives and saw the exhibition displaying many of Roosevelt's papers as well as the surrender documents. After that I walked around the Washington monument but the line was too long to wait so I went to the Lincoln Memorial. From there I walked past the White House, but I did not see Harry. After this I went up town and ate. Now I am writing this as it is still early. I have not decided what I'll do to-night.

That's all for now.

Love,
Donald

Monday, Nov 19, 1945
Aberdeen Proving Ground, M.d.

Dear Mother and Dad,

Just a short note to get you know where I am and that I will be home for Thanksgiving unless something happens between now and then.

When I returned to camp last Tuesday I found that I was on shipping orders for 7:00 that morning. We found that we were to be assigned to several new detachments forming at A P Hill a camp near Belvoir. We did not report to this place but went to another part of Belvoir where we were to attend school for the balance of the week.

On Saturday we shipped to this camp after completing the school at Belvoir on Friday after noon. This took most of the day as we traveled in buses. We began school here today and will be finished by the first of December when we return to Ft. Belvoir or A P Hill to pick up equipment before we move out on a job.

This is supposed to be a pretty good set up as we operate in detachments of eight men and an officer. We will be checking to see that artillery and bombing ranges have been cleared in camps that have been closed so that they may be returned to civilian usage. We will live in towns and be paid five dollars a day for meals and living quarters so this will be a good chance to pick up extra money.

We will get passes at five o'clock on Wednesday so that I will be able to get home some time around nine or ten o'clock. We have to be back by 5:30 Friday morning so that isn't too good. I'll probably be able to get a pass about ten o'clock Saturday morning so that I hope I'll be home in time for Bud's wedding. Did you get the invitation and the present?

Will see you Thursday.

Love,
Donald

Tuesday, Dec 11, 1945
Engineer Board Fort Belvoir Va

Dear Mother and Dad,

How is your Christmas shopping coming along? Do you have most of it finished or are you leaving it until the last minute to finish up the last details and then still forget a few gifts.

I arrived in Washington about 8 o'clock last Monday and was able to check into the service man's hotel near Union Station. On Tuesday morning we all met in the new War Department Building and seeing that the officer that we were to have the conference with had not arrived we adjorned to a nearby restaurant for coffee and doughnuts. After a while we went to the conference which lasted three hours and briefly told us our duties in general terms.

We were then given another pass and told to report to A P Hill in the morning. Kelley and I saw movie and had a late dinner and hit a bed early as we had to be up by four-thirty in order to get the train for the camp.

It rained all that next day so it was none to pleasant a prospect of being in tents. In the afternoon we finally were moved to Ft. Belvoir again so we took passes to Washington and reported to Belvoir in the morning. I am certainly glad I didn't have to spend more than four hours in tents.

Since we have been in Belvoir we have been attempting to set up the detachment and straighten out all the records necessary. We have gotten along fairly well with this and everything should be in good order by next week.

If everything is in good shape by then I should be able to get my Christmas furlough some time during the later part of the week so that I will be home by Friday night at the very latest with an earlier date very possible. The furlough will last until the 3rd of January so that will give me about two weeks at home which is pretty good.

Will close now hoping to see you soon.

Love,
Donald

Miller, Burk,
Ferratti, Holmes
and Vail
at Ft. Belvoir

Vail with Ferratti,
Miller & Holmes
at Ft. Belvoir

Vail and Ferratti
at Ft. Belvoir

Donald Vail
at Valdosta

Feb. 5, 1946
Thomasville AA Field,
Thomasville, Ga

Dear Mother and Dad,

This has been the sunny south land for the past week. We left Atlanta on the 31st, Thursday, after a rainy night but by the time we arrived in Thomasville the sun was out quite strongly. Thomasville is about two-hundred forty miles directly south of Atlanta and about fifty miles north of the Florida line. The weather has been excellent as we have been going around in shirt sleeves and I got quite a sun burn yesterday while we were working out in the field.

We found out that we could live in Valdosta and it would be much closer to the range area that we are clearing. Another team has been working here with us so that we will be finished in another couple of days. Our next job will be down in Florida fairly close to St. Petersburg and Tampa, on the West Coast. We will probably leave here next Monday. The address will be c/o Post Engr.

Pinellas AA Field

St. Petersburg, Fla.

but it is better to use this only in an emergency and continue to use the more permanent address that I sent in my last letter.

I was sorry to hear that you were ill, Mother, and I hope that every one is well at home now.

Thanks for sending the letter from NCE*. They do not have summer refresher courses so I'll try Rutgers perhaps. I'll be able to reenter NCE in the fall without difficulty.

Did you send the watch as yet? Perhaps it would be best to mail the insurance check and then I can return the money by mail order. Enclosed are two mail orders for one hundred dollars each. My back pay finally came thru. I have saved about fifty dollars of this $150 that we get every month for living expense so it isn't too bad.

Love,
Donald

* Newark College of Engineering

Sunday, February 24, 1946
Blumenthal AA Field, Wilmington, N.C.

Dear Mother and Dad,

I received your letter when we were near St. Petersburg. I also received the wrist watch. It is a good thing that you decided to send the check to me as it had a sixty day limit on it. I was able to cash it and get money orders for it which I will enclose in this letter.

As for the watch it has the same thing wrong with it as when I originally got it. It still runs 20 minutes fast to every hour and there is something definitely wrong with it. I'll mail it back to you sometime this week with the hope that the jewelry store will be able to repair it without too much difficulty.

We only spent about four or five day near Saint Petersburg, which was just long enough for us to do the job. The range here at Wilmington have some sort of political backing and so we did not get much time to lie around in the Florida sunshine. I was able to find where Uncle Mac lived but the afternoon that I was able to stop there he was not at home.

I may have to call you for some money to live on if our mail kepts as messed up as it has been for the last two weeks. No one has been able to get a letter as all of the post offices have been sending our mail back to Atlanta no matter whether we have been there or are yet to arrive. In this mail are our checks for $150 so everyone is just about broke but hoping for mail tomorrow.

Hoping to hear from you soon.

Love,
Donald

This was Donald's last letter. His last entry in his travel log was dated February 1946, Wilmington, N.C.

DONALD VAIL IS HOME ON 12 DAY FURLOUGH

Nov. 1943.

Looking as "rugged as a Kansas farmer" according to his mother, Pfc. Donald B. Vail, son of Mr. and Mrs. Harvey Vail of New Market, arrived home unexpectedly Sunday on a 12-day furlough. He is stationed at Concordia, Kansas, where he is doing guard duty at a prison camp. A graduate of Dunellen High School, Donald studied two years at the Newark College of Engineering, and now has his application in for the special training program in mechanical engineering. There will be a family gathering at the Vail home Sunday in his honor. He entered the service last June and received his basic training at Fort Custer, Michigan.

PLAINFIELD, N. J., COURIER-NEWS, FRIDAY, DECEMBER 1, 1944

ARRIVES IN ENGLAND—Pfc. Donald B. Vail, son of Mr. and Mrs. Harvey A. Vail of 377 Vail Ave., New Market, who has arrived in England with the Army Engineers.

Pfc. Donald B. Vail Now in England With Engineers

New Market—Pfc. Donald B. Vail has arrived in England with the Army Combat Engineers, according to word received by his parents, Mr. and Mrs. Harvey A. Vail of 377 Vail Ave.

He was inducted into the Army June 4, 1943, and trained at Fort Custer, Mich., with the military police. He was sent to Concordia, Kan., to guard German prisoners of war.

Accepted later for the Army Specialized Training program, he was assigned to the University of Tennessee. From there he went to Camp Crowder, Missouri, and later was assigned to the Engineers at Camp Rucker, Alabama.

Private Vail took a 12-week course in mechanics at the Atlanta Ordnance School, Atlanta, Ga., from where he was graduated Sept. 1. He was graduated from Dunellen High School and attended Newark College of Engineering.

Corp. Donald Vail

Corp. Donald Vail Home on Furlough

New Market—Corp. Donald Vail, son of Mr. and Mrs. Harvey Vail, 377 Vail Ave., arrived home recently on a 30-day furlough, after serving approximately one year in the European Theater.

Corporal Vail, who arrived in this country on Friday aboard the USS "Victory," has been in service since June 4, 1943. He received his basic training at Fort Custer, Mich., and later was transferred to Concordia, Kans., where he served as a member of the escort guard. Following this, he received ASTP training at the University of Tennessee, and then was stationed in Camp Crowder, Mo., and later in Alabama, after which he was sent to the European Theater on Oct. 22, 1944. He served successively with the Ninth and 15th Armies in England, Holland, Germany, France and Belgium.

Articles about Donald in the local paper, The Plainfield N.J. Courier-News

Epilogue

Following his discharge and return home to Dunellen, New Jersey, Donald resumed his studies at the Newark College of Engineering. It was in Dunellen, that his cousin Norma Schlunsen (photo with letter dated June 25, 1944) introduced Donald to his future wife, Betty Lou Keates.

Post-war 1948 was an eventful year for Donald. He graduated from the Newark College of Engineering and received a Bachelors of Science degree in Mechanical Engineering with full honors, was hired by the General Electric Company in Schenectady, New York, and, in that same year, married Betty Lou in October. They set up house and lived in Schenectady until 1956.

Transferring with GE to San Jose, California that year, Donald and Betty Lou moved with their then three children (Diane, Donald Jr. "Barry" and Cynthia) and settled on the West Coast. Their fourth child (Shelley) was born in San Jose. Donald spent his entire career with GE concluding it as a mechanical engineer in the Nuclear Energy Division. He retired in 1989.

Betty Lou died in San Jose November of 2001. Donald died 6 months later. He was 78 years old.

Donald B. Vail, Jr.
March 2022

Appendix 1

A portion of Donald's Mother's response concerning D-Day. This was referenced in the Postcard post-marked June 13,1944.

June 6th 1944

Dear Donald:-

Well D-Day found me at the church before 11 a.m. and again in the evening to a devotional service planned by Mr. Palmer for the members of the Nagle Bible Class and any others that happened to stop in, such as myself.

Shortly after I arrived, Aunt Clara and Aunt Nete came in and quietly took their seats. I was seated in the front pew as near the "Honor Roll" (which Mr. Palmer placed on the communion table between two candle sticks in which were lighted candles) as I could get and was surprised when I turned my head to see Neve & Clara. Soon after, Dot Adams came in and sat next to me.

Mr. Palmer was very faithful to what he felt was his duty. He rang the church bells every hour. In fact it was the ringing of the bells that awakened me out of a deep sleep to the realization that it was D-Day. I immediately jumped out of bed and got dressed and went over. Everybody seemed to be tense and rather nervous. I cancelled my plans to attend the B & P club's picnic supper at the Scharf Estate in N. Pfd because I felt it was a time to spend in prayer and meditation, rather than fun....

Love,
Mother and Dad

Appendix 2

Mother's first response to Donald's letter requesting money to be sent in order to purchase an engagement ring for "the one". See telegram after July 30, 1944 letter.

Thursday August 10, 1944
Dunellen, New Jersey

Dear Donald,

Hold everything!!! The money will be wired to you as soon as Dad can withdraw it. Presume it will be used to purchase the engagement ring for "the one" you spoke of.

To become engaged is one thing, but to make a hasty marriage would be too bad.

Take plenty of time to think it over before making the fatal plunge into matrimony, as it is much more difficult to get out of, than to get into.

Those Georgia belle's have a way of making a man's head swim, with their charming manners and Southern accent, and if it is a Georgia girl, I'm sure I don't blame you for falling hard, but, remember that the Southern girls will find it hard to be contented up North after the war is over.

Dad and I shall never stand in the way of your happiness, but it will be a source of joy and comfort to us, to know that you have the right woman, which is the only means of real happiness for man.

Try to put the phone call thru on Sunday afternoon between 2 and 3 P.M. as I have to go to the "At Ease" Center on the 5 P.M. bus.

I am supposed to have one night a week off which is Monday, usually. But this past Monday I had to work as the lady who substitutes for me is on vacation.

Well, wonders will never cease. We'll be anxious to know more about the girl, and to see her, or a picture of her.

I always thought you were the slow, bashful type, but I have changed my mind.

With lots of love and best wishes,
Mother & Dad

Appendix 3

Second letter from Mother regarding "the one". After letter dated August 10, 1944.

Monday, August 14th '44
Dunellen, New Jersey

Dearest Donald,

I do hope that you have forgiven me for being so sharp over the telephone, but you know that is my only defense in time of tears, and I have shed plenty since receiving your letter.

It is the most natural thing in the world for parents to protect their young, and that is all Dad and I are anxious to do. We both want you to get the most happiness out of life, and if you feel that the only way you can ever hope to be happy is by marrying Paulette, then, we shall leave everything in your hands, and pray that God in his wisdom, will guide you are right in making this, your greatest decision in life, a wise one, and that everything will turn out just as you and Paulette wish.

We feel sure Paulette must be everything you say she is, and perhaps more, and you know it is our desire that you both enjoy life to the fullest extent, but we want you both to think the matter over very seriously, due to the difference in religion, and the effect it may have on your offspring, if any.

Youth is so absorbed in the things of the present, that it gives little or no thought to the future and the disastrous results which very often are inevitable following a hasty marriage.

You know, Donald, that your happiness has been upper most in our minds and we do not want to stand in the way of it now, at this most crucial period of your life.

From the time you take the marriage vows, you realize you are on your own, and must do everything in your power to protect your wife, and look out for her happiness.

It isn't an easy thing for parents to part with their children, especially an only child, knowing full well that everything we had ever hoped for and dreamed of his wrapped up in that child, but that is the way of life.

We know that we shall gain a daughter, but it is a source of great joy and satisfaction if everything is harmonious all around.

Since you are both so young, and so daring, to plunge into matrimony on such short acquaintance we beg of you to do nothing without the consent of Paulette's mother. everything hinges on that, you know as things may become very complicated without it.

Trusting that you received the $100 dad wired on Sunday afternoon August 13 and that everything will work out satisfactorily for all concerned.

I may see you before Friday if I can make the necessary arrangements here.

Until then; with love and best wishes for your happiness,

Love and kisses,
Mother and Dad

Appendix 4

A letter from Mother and Dad upon his being sent to Europe

Tuesday October 24th 1944

Dear Donald,

It was so nice to get the card and to know that you are still around although I can imagine how uneasy you must feel not knowing when or where you will be each day. The anticipation is much harder to bear than the realization. Of course you know we are anxious to see you again before you leave, if that is possible, but, if not, we'll just have to make the best of it until you do return, and that can't be too soon to suit us. Drop us a line again, if you possibly can. Even a postal card is better than nothing. If you should stay away too long, you know I'm apt to join the WACs or something in hopes of following you up. The whole thing seems so adventuresome and a bit unreal, that you should be following in your father's footsteps and perhaps cover the same territory he covered some twenty-five years ago with a great deal more added to it.

One might consider it the opportunity of a lifetime seeing what the rest of the world looks like, but it is too bad to think that that opportunity has to come under such awful circumstances.

You'll be on your own over there and we beg of you to be careful, don't take any risks just for the sake of a medal. And, whatever you do, keep good company both male and female? If and when you need sympathetic understanding, look up your chaplain. You'll find him very good company, I'm sure, and always ready to be of help spiritually and otherwise. I don't mean to preach it is just good sound advice!

To change the subject, Junior and one of his boy friends came Sunday afternoon to take two sections of plywood for the table he wants to build in his room. He sold his electric trains to a friend of Uncle Wes' for $50 and he went to the Cran's shop and bought the HO model engine and other cars amounting to $55. Then he came here and bought 10 (cents) worth of spikes for his track. He has the craze just like you once had. I do not intend to sell your engine or small cars as I want to keep them in remembrance of the long hours you devoted to the work. Someday you may have children that would enjoy these things. Also it is almost if not impossible to get the engines now, which makes them all the more valuable. We haven't decided what to charge Junior for the plywood. What would you suggest?

Well, Raoul had a birthday Saturday and I'm wondering if he really intends to sign up. He is doing so well at the Diner, it does seem too bad to hurry into something uncertain.

We are happy to know you enjoyed the cake and other good things and if I can get away with it, I'll try to mail you a box every week or ten days and include cheese and crackers and etc.

Take care of yourself, and keep happy, no matter what happens. We'll be with you in spirit, even though we cannot be with you in the flesh.

With all our love and kisses,
Mother and Dad

Appendix 5

A partial Letter from Mother to Donald, in Europe, following the death of President Roosevelt.

Thursday evening.
April 12, 1945

Dear Donald:
Well the world is aflame tonight, I'm sure, with the news of the President's sudden death. Of course, I wasn't exactly shocked to hear it as I have felt for some time that he was failing very fast. It was very noticeable in his speech to Congress upon his return from the Yalta Conf.

He remained seated during that report to Congress, and I noticed a definite slowness in speech, which I attributed to physical weakness.

I suppose, I too, mourn with the rest of the nation because of the awful mess which remains to be settled at the peace table without his able assistance. I attended the library board meeting tonight, and overheard uncle Carl mutter under his breath something about him being a Gestapo chief referring to F.D. I imagine.

Of course, I admired his courage in fighting his affliction; his knowledge of the world affairs and maybe a few other things, but there were many things I disliked too.

Perhaps someday, we'll know whether or not he did the right thing by sending our young men into battle to be sacrificed for what? Nobody knows as yet.

I wonder how Mrs. Smith across the street a democrat feels, as she happens to be a gold star mother, now. And he died of his wounds, received on Iwo Jima, no doubt on March 3 and was buried on Guam on March 4. She received a letter telling of the funeral service held for him. The letter stated that he was dressed in his white sailor suit and eight boys in white acted as guard of honor.

Mrs. Smith is very sad and finds it difficult to concentrate on anything.

While the rest of the nation mourns over FDR's death, my sympathy goes out to the families of the fine young men that are giving their lives for us. That, to me, is much more tragic than even the death of a president. I'm entitled to my opinion, am I not?

Appendix 6

A letter from Mother following V-J Day

Saturday Evening
August 17, 1945

Dear Donald:

Well, the long awaited V-J day has come and gone. The world went wild for a couple of days at least; and I do hope things will work out as anticipated, as far as we and the Japs are concerned.

Dad had a two day holiday, and I had Thursday off with pay, as well as receiving double pay for working Wednesday. The telephone company belongs to the union, hence the double time for working the two holidays, which the president declared by mistake, so they are trying to claim, now.

We had a wonderful time in N. Y. on Thursday. We got an early start and took in Radio City (over 21) which was very good, and of course, a fine floor show. After the show, we went to Shraft's for lunch and then took a bus ride up Fifth Avenue to 160th St. to see the sights, then back to Washington Square, where we got off and walked through the Italian section, which was gaily decorated with small American flags above the streets, as well as flags of all the allied nations, also bright, colored streamers, hanging from fire escapes on the tenement houses. Men, women, and children filled the streets. The children laughing with glee, while the old men and boys sat around in groups, either playing cards while drinking beer, or playing crap. Most of the women folk were hanging out the windows talking to the neighbors. The scene reminded me of the book, "A Tree Grows in Brooklyn" only, we were in New York. From there, we walked on until we reached 'China Town.' That was something to remember. First of all we came upon a block dance where we saw American girls, as well as girls of other nationalities, dancing with Chinese soldiers and sailors. For that matter, all of the young people were American born. There were some pretty good looking Chinamen in ChinaTown. We walked around another street and watched the Chinamen gather for a parade which one Chinamen told me, lasted all night, and in fact, had been going on for three nights. As the orchestra, which consisted of a drum, and two brass symbols, or whatever they choose to call those tin things, played a monotonous tune, a Chinaman appeared from a doorway, with a monstrous dragon head held over his head. It is called a dragon of Peace, I believe. A couple of Chinese boys with large papier-mâché heads over their heads, lead the way, beckoning the people to follow the dragon. A large group of China men of all ages, some dressed in their native dress, followed the dragon, which goes into some sort of rapturous dance, and suddenly a pack of firecrackers shoot off, to add to the merriment. I suppose the custom dates back two thousand years. Maybe they all get drunk before morning. We didn't hang around long enough to find out. We visited a couple of the shops and bought a few souvenirs. We then took the subway train back to City Hall, where we stopped at Child's for a bite to eat, and arrived home about 11 P. M. Lucky thing I had Friday off, also, as I was dead tired, after all that walking around New York.

We thought of you all the while, and wondered if you were given time off to celebrate.

I worked two hours overtime at the hospital the night the President made the announcement, arriving home just as the whistles started blowing, and automobiles were racing and tearing like mad around street corners, blowing horns, and the people shouting at everybody else. Mrs. Joseph stood out in front of her place ringing a New Year's bell, and hugging and kissing all the men that drove in for gas. She was like a wild woman. Of course it means more business for her, now. Why shouldn't she be happy? I haven't seen Mrs. Mikus to talk to, but I know she is the happiest person in the neighborhood. I imagine Mrs. Krug must be, too. Mrs. Smith was happy it was over, too, but she will never get over Andy's death. She cries all the time.

Our happiness knew no bounds, as I'm sure you'll be coming home much sooner than you had expected, don't you think?

I was talking to a fellow from the Panther division who said he met up with the 288Th Eng. at Coblenz. In fact, I think he said he worked with them for a while. Do you recall it? Another boy with whom I talk to, while he was waiting for his call to go thru, said he work with your outfit at Worms. He belonged to the Triple A Gun Batt. Battery C, 214th Artillery. Correction, please.

It was at Metz. His name is John R. Terpack and he got quite well acquainted with fellows by the name of Charles Statts, Owensburg, Ky. and Maxi Sneed, Madisonville, Ky. Are they in your outfit?

It is so nice to talk with the fellows who have met up with your outfit. It seems to bring you closer to home, because I feel sure you'll be following close behind, I hope. When you do get home, I'll take a month off, like some of the other women have done. I have worked for the past three Sundays as well as quite some over-time. By the time they deduct the tax, I don't have too much to show for my efforts, but I certainly do enjoy the work, even though it tires me out at times. The housework is falling behind, as usual, but the work won't go on many more months, then I can stay home and houseclean for a change. Maybe I'll enjoy it, who knows?

Is there anything in particular you would like for Christmas, just in case you are not lucky enough to get home in time? I believe the boxes are to be shipped the 15th of October this year, unless they change it again. I hope Lew Kirchner won't have to stay over there a year. Marguerite misses him so much. She looks so thin, and so sad.

Edna has her hands full for looking after the two kids all by herself. Maybe they'll release the married men with children. I think they should, don't you?

Well, here's hoping you return home well, and happy, before long. What do you say we take a couple of rooms in one of the expensive Hotels in N.Y. and really celebrate in a big way. I'll start saving some of my checks. You've got a nice fat bank account with insurance money falling due the first of the year, I think. Let's buy a car, and I need a new refrigerator. The darn thing went dead on us. The man came today to look at it, and he said it would cost 60 or 80 dollars to buy a new unit. So I guess we'll hold tight and turn it in toward another one. I'd like a new gas range, too, and lots of things.

Well, here it is Tuesday, and I'm still on this letter. We are having a hot spell again. So between the heat and the after affects of V-J Day, I have slowed down considerably. I talked with a soldier who had just returned Sunday night (an engineer who claims he was stationed on the beach in South Wales, while you (288th Eng.) were there. His A. P. O. was 134. Remember? I suppose I'll continue to meet fellows who have seen your outfit, or have worked side-by-side with you.

If you should return sooner than you expect, and should come to Kilmer, go to a coin booth at one of the telephone exchanges and call " official 29" & find out if I'm working. They'll tell you what exchange I'm at. You'll be stationed there about 24 hrs. before leaving for Dix. If you return on one of the large ships, you are destined to arrive at Kilmer. I sure hope so.

Dad and I are looking forward to your early return.

With lots of love and kisses,
Mother and Dad

Appendix 7

A letter to Donald from his friend in the A.S.T.P., Pvt. Edward M. Pyatt, Jr. (Ed Pyatt)

Washington University, St. Louis, Missouri
11 February 1944

Dear Don,

Well I see you finally made it. I was a little worried for you with all the rumors of closing A.S T. floating around. They sure are raising hell with our outfit. Lots of fellows in Term III are get shipping orders before the end of the term although they are getting credit for the work. Fellows are going right and left on failures.

The work seems pretty easy to me— probably because I've had everything but the physics at Drexel.

How do you like Knoxville. From what I have heard it's a pretty good city. A fellow from Drexel was there in the A/C's and another is or was in A. S. T. His last name is Rixse. Oh hell Don— I just looked up the letter and it's Nashville not Knoxville. I'm FUBAR again as usual.

Anyway the hell with it. St. Louis suits me perfectly. It's a swell city and the people are O. K. I'm running around with a junior in Bus. Ad. here who is positively delectable. My roommate goes with another girl, her cousin who lives only a couple of blocks from the school. She has her own car and believe me we don't let any Saturday nights or Sundays go to waste.

Before I forget it you had better get out your little black book and change my address to what it is on the envelope. Then I won't have to chase all over hell for my mail. And don't forget I was busted in Sacramento.

I hope to get a furlough in three weeks and give the old home town going over with a couple of days in Philadelphia and Indianapolis.

Let me know how things are going and how you like education at a gallop.

Your Pal,

Ed

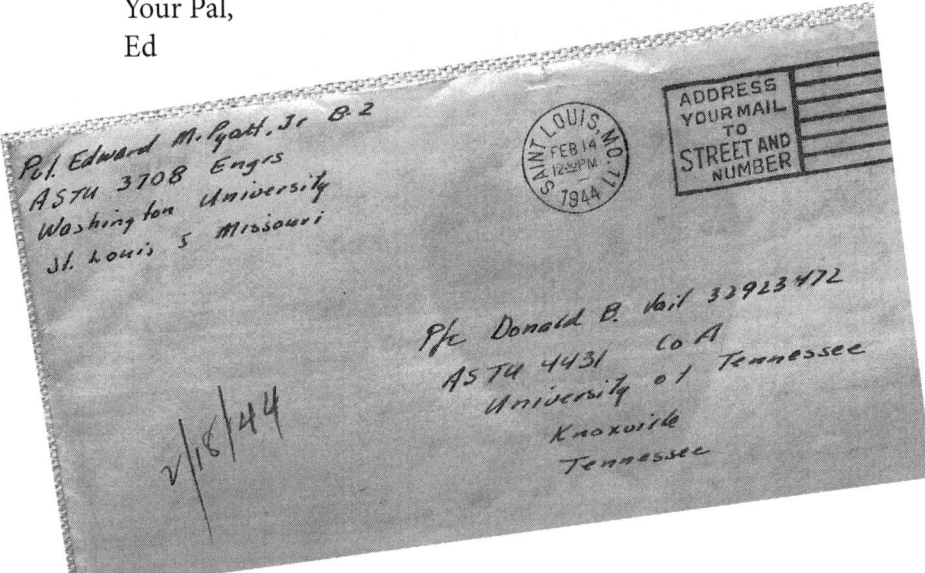

Appendix 8

A letter from Donald's friend, Marion Dempster, written on lined paper in pencil.

West Orange, New Jersey
February18, 1944

Dear Donald,

    Our letters seem to cross one another every time we write. I sent one to your old address which by now you probably have received. First before I go any further I will explain to you why I am writing in pencil and on this paper. I have spare time on my hands at work and I thought this would be a good time to catch up on my correspondence so here goes.

    I was sorry to hear that your friend's mother passed away. I hope you didn't find it too difficult to write a letter to him. I would like to thank you very much for the patches you sent me they are different from the one I have which is from the air corp. I received a bottle of perfume & an (?) from a friend in Texas and it arrived on Valentine's Day which was very appropriate.

    We have had quite a mild winter except for a couple of days which we had snow last week. We had quite a snowfall about 8 inches and it was swell.

    I went to New York Sunday with two of my girlfriends and we saw the Prudential Hour broadcast it was excellent and afterwards we went to Child's for dinner. I looked for the one we went to, but i'll be darned if I could find it. Maybe you can tell me where it is so if we go again I will be able to find the place. I am going skating Saturday night for the first time in months. I don't think I will remember how to skate. The fellow next-door is back in the US after being in Alaska for two years he is finally back. I guess he won't want to do much when he gets home.

    Well, Don I don't have much news this trip but I'll try to store some up for the next letter.

    Please excuse the pencil but no ink was available.

    As Ever,
    Marion

Appendix 9

A letter to Donald from his friend, Pvt. Jos. Houska (Joe)
Chanute Field, Rantoul, Ill.

April, 22, '45

Dear Don,

By now you must be regarding your "old buddy" as a lowly turd! For months I've been writing you a mental letter and don't quite know how to apologize for the results that "ain't ever showed up."

Sometime back I hoped for some further news following receipt of your APO address. Quite a bit must have been forced on your life since then & I pray this little missile still finds you at least enjoying good health.

My progress towards an overseas assignment has been somewhat delayed a number of times. During these instances the sound of tramping feet has come mighty close and I've sweated out the transfers to the infantry. Some of my friends have kept me posted on that IRTC deal and one recently received the Purple Heart.

At present I am completing a radar course here at Chanute. While a lot of bitching always highlights tech school training, the work itself has been interesting. Still, it won't be too soon 'fore the millions of us guys can return to things which had to be put aside for the duration.

Don, some of my boys have come for that date to town so I'll toss down a few for you, while I'm at it.

Meanwhile take care of yourself—€ and I'll answer your next letter immediately upon arrival!

Your old Dunellen heartthrob,
Houska

Appendix 10

A letter from Donald's friend, C. B. Thatcher, Jr. (Bud)

August 5th, 1945
Childress, Texas

Hi Don,

Just got back to Childress after about 10 days at home to find your letter waiting for me. Don't blow your top because it wasn't a leave this time, but ostensibly a delay in route to Lincoln, Nebraska. But on arriving home I found a telegram canceling the orders and telling me to return to see C. A. A. F. at the end of the delay. Right now I am assigned here for about a week until I leave for Lincoln— this time I hope I get there. That field is the Army Air Forces Combat Crew Processing Center and from there crews are sent to R. T. U. centers and hence overseas. Most of the guys think I'm crazy for volunteering to go back but I can't see any percentage in just hanging around these redeployment schools. Actually it will be at least six months before I get overseas and I'm quite sure that between now and then something will happen to my health— if you know what I mean.

Had the usual swell time while I was home spending 99.9% of the time at Jeanie's place— you remember the girl from Fanwood, don't you? Really miss the gal. We had intended to get married quite a while ago but have been continually putting it off. Actually I am more responsible than Jeanie because I hate the thought of a wife and being broke.

Suppose you know that Johnny Probicky was listed as M.I.A. in a B-29 after a raid Japan. Went around and called on his mother while I was home. Hope for the best but actually I am not too hopeful because there isn't very much in the line of an underground that can help you out in that neck of the woods.

The discharge situation is still very rough at least on this field. Points still mean very little. You should know better than to question the derivation of my 83 points. Hells bells, in the air Corps you get medals for meritorious service in the latrine— if you don't fall in. You know that. Realize that your position is pretty bad— personally I would rather stay in the Army of Occupation in the E.T. O. rather than go to the Pacific.

Had to sell my car for several reasons. Primarily I couldn't take it with me to my next station but I also needed the dough. These leaves with my expensive tastes really cost plenty. Once you have a car it really is hard to get along without one – you certainly must know that from your experience with your Chevie.

Take it easy,
Bud

Appendix 11

A letter from Donald's friend, Lt. Ernest A. Mikus (Ernie Mikus) typewritten on V-Mail

APO 350 ETOa
6 August '45

Dear Donald,

Received your letter of the 24th July yesterday as I returned from a little week trip to the big city of Paris. I had been sent there for the I&E school that they held there. It was a pretty nice deal with living at the City University and having all of our nights free. This was my first trip to Paris and it was a swell vacation.

I also received your letter that you had written to me at Rheinberg. It took a little time to get here but better late than never as they say. I certainly wish that I were back in Germany for that would certainly be the deal now. The matter of fraternization is no longer the 65 dollar question. From what I have heard the boys are really going after the German frauleins or more correctly vica versa.

I feel certain that I will not see you in the ETO Donald for you are in the American sector of occupation and there is no way that I can get out there. As you can guess our time is running out rather rapidly and before long we should be going up the gang plank, only as I explained to you in my last letter I will not see 7th and Washington— well that is the way it goes but I can't complain for I haven't been over too long and so going to the Pacific does not bother me too much. In the long run I honestly believe that it is the short way home.

Ed Gornick wrote me the other day that he has just been sent to the Philippines after knocking about the Solomons and other God forsaken places for quite a while. From what he said it was not so bad. At any rate I imagine that life with an EG company will not be too bad. Ed sent me some pictures of the black "belles" of the Solomons and as you can guess they were really beauties— in a gruesome sort of way. Before long I should have a chance to see for myself.

As you probably know Joe is home for good on a medical discharge. From what he told me his vision is not impaired too badly in that one eye. He made me sick as he wrote me of going to Plainfield and buying sport jackets and all sorts of sport clothes. He will go back to Rutgers in the fall and so things should not be too bad for him. It certainly must be great to be in civilian clothes—I bet we all will feel strange for a while; however, I am willing to try. I rather guessed that you would too.

Your letter mentioned that you have shipping lists staring you in the face. Does that mean that they are breaking your outfit up to use as replacements? There is one thing that I don't like about sitting in occupied territory and that is the possibility of being stuck in the occupation end of this war. That is something that I want no part of. For now I just hope that this mess in the pacific ends rather soon so that we can go to dear old Dunellen and start living.

Please excuse this sloppy typing donald but I had some shots in the arm this afternoon and my arm feels a little numb. So for now I'll say so long. Please let me hear from you soon so that I can find out what's new with you.

As ever
Ernie

Acknowledgements

This compilation is completed at the encouragement of friends and family for which I am deeply grateful.

I want to acknowledge the efforts of my wife, Allison who proofread my transcriptions of Dad's letters, and designed and produced the manuscript. Without her work this project would never have seen the light of day. Thanks also to niece, Heather Ehlert, who offered Allison consultation in computer and program needs for the production of this book. Thanks also to Isaac Vail for other technical assistance and to Hannah E. V. Stitzlein for editorial assistance.